Beyond Betrayal

"All will be well, all will be
well, and all manner of
things will be well."
Julian of Norwich

Anna-Marie,
With great admiration, appreciation
and affection.
Patty

Beyond Betrayal

The Priest Sex Abuse Crisis, the Voice of the Faithful, and the Process of Collective Identity

PATRICIA EWICK AND
MARC W. STEINBERG

The University of Chicago Press   Chicago and London

The University of Chicago Press, Chicago 60637
The University of Chicago Press, Ltd., London
© 2019 by The University of Chicago
Published 2019
Printed in the United States of America

28 27 26 25 24 23 22 21 20 19   1 2 3 4 5

ISBN-13: 978-0-226-64412-7 (cloth)
ISBN-13: 978-0-226-64426-4 (paper)
ISBN-13: 978-0-226-64443-1 (e-book)
DOI: https://doi.org/10.7208/chicago/9780226644431.001.0001

Library of Congress Cataloging-in-Publication Data

Names: Ewick, Patricia, author. | Steinberg, Marc W. (Marc William),
    1956– author.
Title: Beyond betrayal : the priest sex abuse crisis, the Voice Of The
    Faithful, and the process of collective identity / Patricia Ewick and
    Marc W. Steinberg.
Description: Chicago : The University of Chicago Press, 2019. | Includes
    bibliographical references and index.
Identifiers: LCCN 2019001389 | ISBN 9780226644127 (cloth : alk. paper) |
    ISBN 9780226644264 (pbk. : alk. paper) | ISBN 9780226644431 (e-book)
Subjects: LCSH: Child sexual abuse by clergy—Massachusetts—Boston. |
    St. Erasmus VOTF. | Voice of the Faithful (Organization) | Catholic
    Church—Massachusetts—Societies, etc. | Catholics—Religious
    identity—Massachusetts.
Classification: LCC BX1912.9.E95 2019 | DDC 282/.744—dc23
LC record available at https://lccn.loc.gov/2019001389

♾ This paper meets the requirements of ANSI/NISO Z39.48–1992
(Permanence of Paper).

We dedicate this book to the memory of past members of the St. Erasmus VOTF and to those still involved in keeping the faith and changing the church.

Contents

Acknowledgments

This book has been a long time in the making. We would like to thank the following friends and colleagues for their ideas, support, and generosity: Nancy Whittier, Steve Boutcher, and the rest of the Five College Social Movement Group; Lee Cuba, Susan Silbey, Kristin Bumiller, Alice Hearst, Martha Minow, Martha Umphreys, Patricia Williams, and Shelly Tenebaum. We would also like to express our gratitude to Deborah Gould and David Smilde for offering venues to present our ongoing work. We also thank the staffs of the Clark University and Smith College libraries.

A special thanks to our editors Doug Mitchell and Elizabeth Branch Dyson, whose encouragement and support was critical as we finished the book. A note of thanks to Kyle Wagner at the University of Chicago Press for shepherding the project.

Above all we express our greatest thanks to the St. Erasmus Voice of the Faithful. For the past twelve years they shared their stories with us, included us in their meetings, conferences, commemorations, and celebrations. They invited us into their homes and introduced us to their families. One would think after twelve years they would have pressured us to finish. They never did. Perhaps more than most they understand that some things take longer than you expect. Without their wisdom, generosity, and candor, this book would not have been written. Norms of confidentiality and anonymity prevent us from naming them. But they know who they are. Thank you.

PART ONE

The Scandal:
Rebuilding a Boat at Sea

"At least I have launched this big ship. Another will have the task of taking it out to sea." POPE JOHN XXIII[1]

On January 7, 2013, a group of twenty people assembled in the community hall in the basement of St. Erasmus Roman Catholic Church in Massachusetts to commemorate what one of them referred to as "Revelation Day." Eleven years earlier, on January 6, 2002, the *Boston Globe* published the first of a series of reports on the archdiocese cover-up of sexual abuse by priests. The banner headline told a tragic story that would, in its basic plot, be repeated with disturbing regularity over the course of the next decade: "Church Allowed Abuse by Priest for Years: Aware of Geoghan Record, Archdiocese Still Shuttled Him from Parish to Parish." Many Catholics would leave the Church as a result of the sexual abuse scandal; many would remain staunchly faithful, denying any sort of a systematic cover-up. Some Catholics—among them those who assembled in the basement of St. Erasmus—would decide to keep their faith, but also to change the Church. They called themselves the St. Erasmus Affiliate of Voice of the Faithful, or St. Erasmus VOTF. They had been meeting every Monday night for eleven years.

One of the most stalwart members present that night was Sister Bridget Deignan. Sister Bridget was a seventy-five-year-old nun, or a "woman religious" as they are now known. Her age and vocation do not conjure the woman, however. She is a self-avowed feminist and supports the ordination of women and the elimination of mandatory celibacy for priests. Unlike the stock stories of stern nuns, Bridget is incredibly gracious and kind and has a mischievous sense of humor. Speaking about the possibility that someday a new pastor of St. Erasmus parish might not allow the VOTF affiliate to meet in the basement, Bridget observed with a smile and a wink, "Boy, he'd be in trouble—write whoever it was a sympathy note."

Bridget decided at the age of seventeen that she was called by God to become a nun. Her early years in the convent were traditional. As a member of a religious order, she took a religious name. Bridget was now called Carmella, wore a long habit, and rose every morning at 5:25 for Mass, prayer, and meditation. She would do her chores, or "charges." According to Bridget, most women in religious life at the time taught school and did housework.

The settled life that Bridget was living was to be irrevocably changed. In October 1962, Pope John XXIII convened the Second Vatican Council (also known as "Vatican II"), one of the most important religious events of the twentieth century. Against the active resistance of the Roman Curia, or the Vatican bureaucracy, Pope John envisioned the Council as an opportunity for *aggiornamento*, or updating (Wilde 2007). Much of the updating involved aligning the Church with aspects of modernity, and chief among these was the role of the laity in religious life. In particular, the adoption of the vernacular Mass and the reorientation of the altar to face the parish transformed the Mass to be more inclusive of lay Catholics. Rather than mere spectators of a sacrament performed in Latin, a language few parishioners knew, they were now recognized as active participants. Most important, Vatican II "displaced the supremacy of the Church hierarchy as the 'producer' of Catholicism and offered a more egalitarian and culturally dynamic understanding of the production of religious meanings" (Dillon 1999, 25). For many of the faithful— some rapidly, others more gradually—this meant going *beyond* life in the Church as they had practiced it from their youngest memories.

The tectonic changes that came with Vatican II led Bridget and some of her fellow sisters to ask whether there were other ways of leading a religious life. She began reading theology and wondering whether the cloistered, communal life was all there was, or might be, to her vocation. "It looked like religious life needed to be reimagined. We were living the way people had way back in the French Revolution." In particular, Bridget was drawn to parish ministry. She wanted to get a house, live among laypeople, and get involved in the life of the parish. Bridget and four other nuns shed their long habits and rented an apartment, furnishing it with donations from family and friends. Bridget encountered stiff resistance from others in her order, one of whom chastised her by saying that "any sister who wants to show her legs should go home." But she didn't—she made a new home, this time in the community, attending lectures at the Paulist Center, a liberal-leaning Catholic information center run by a small religious order whose slogan was "Missionaries to Main Street"; running a series in the parish on the new liturgy ushered in by Vatican II; and generally redefining what it meant to be a woman religious (Carroll 2009, 34). Reflecting on this time, Bridget sounded wistful: "Something new was adrift." When asked whether she had a sense at that time where this transformation might lead, Bridget observed, "No. You see, it's the same kind of thing with Voice of the Faithful now. You know that something's got to change. And you try to do whatever needs to be done at the moment, hoping that this movement is toward where you're not even sure you want to go."

In 2002, when the sex scandal broke, Bridget had been working in the community for over twenty years. She was shocked by the events and held her most scathing judgment for the members of the church hierarchy who had known about the sexual abuse but shuffled the abusers from parish to parish. For Sister Bridget, the primacy that the hierarchy placed on the good name of the institution rather than on the safety of children was the most egregious injustice, and she was convinced that if women had been in positions of authority it would not have happened. When asked how the sex crisis affected her faith, Bridget said that before the crisis, "I was more simplistic, maybe more idealistic. But I think I'm more real now. I guess my faith in God is deeper." She attributes this deepening of faith to the sense that she is working with others in protecting the Church—and she is clear what she means by the Church. "My definition of 'church' is from Vatican II. We are the people. *We* are the Church." Bridget's use of "we" deliberately included lay Catholics, parish priests, and women religious. Referring to the Roman Catholic Curia, the bishops and cardinals who ruled the Church from the Vatican, she asserted, "If I mean 'hierarchy,' I use 'hierarchy' or 'leadership.' When I say 'Church,' I'm talking about all of us." Always charitable, she added, "including *them.*"

Bridget's activism is infused with the mystery of the divine. This was nowhere more apparent than in her account of how she originally came to a meeting of the Voice of the Faithful. Having heard about a group meeting in Wellesley, Massachusetts, soon after the scandal broke, she and four other parishioners from St. Erasmus decided to attend the weekly listening session. Not knowing what to expect and a little apprehensive, they decided to go to "case the joint," as she mischievously put it. The spring evening was, Bridget recalled, quiet and calm. But after they got out of the car in the crowded Wellesley parking lot, their ambivalence about attending was defeated when "a strong wind came out of nowhere and pushed us toward the door." When they entered the hall—already full with hundreds of people—they "felt fire," she said.

References to direct experiences of the sacred are relatively unusual among the regular members of St. Erasmus VOTF, including Bridget. Despite her devotion and religious vocation, Bridget speaks of her faith quietly, thoughtfully, and with the emotional restraint typical of Bostonians, or the wry humor and skepticism of Irish Catholics. Reflecting this amalgam of faith and reason, tradition and modernity, Bridget's story about the wind and fire was told with wonderment, but it was wonderment laced with a bit of self-consciousness—as if to readily acknowledge that one does not routinely encounter the Holy Spirit in parking lots. Clearly, the presence of the Holy Spirit was felt that evening, even while the invocation of that felt presence was a bit hesitant. Indeed, as Bridget recounted the sense of being pushed by the wind and ignited by the fire, another member, Sarah Fauteux, stepped in to relieve the self-consciousness by good-naturedly joking, "That night we had wind and fire, but what about earth?"

The ambivalence Bridget and her companions felt on that spring evening was not unusual. When the *Boston Globe* story first broke about John Geoghan, many Catholics in the Boston area believed it was an aberrant case. Some believed the stories about the cover-up were exaggerations, evidence of what they saw as the anti-Catholic bias of the *Boston Globe*. But as the evidence of the scope of the abuse and cover-up mounted, these familiar stories of bad-apple priests and biased reporting became unsustainable. It would eventually come to light that John Geoghan had victimized hundreds of boys, some as young as four years old, by gaining the trust of the children's parents, often a single mother who welcomed the attention of the parish priest. The situation soon escalated. In the first four months of 2002, 176 priests were accused of sexual abuse (Investigative Staff of the *Boston Globe* 2002, 5).

As horrifying as these reports of clerical abuse were, it would still have been possible to attribute the number of cases to a lot of individual bad apples. Earlier cases of serial priest abuse in the 1980s and 1990s—in Louisiana, Minneapolis–St. Paul, and even in Boston—did not yield the sort of evidence of systematic cover-up that was so starkly revealed in 2002. What distinguished the Boston 2002 case from prior reports of serial sexual abuse by priests was the revelation of the Church hierarchy's knowledge and cover-up of the crimes—and what could be construed as its collusion in providing new victims to the sexual predators by reassigning the guilty priests to other parishes where many would resume their pattern of abuse. As a report by the Attorney General of Massachusetts was to conclude later that July, "There is overwhelming evidence that for many years Cardinal Law and his senior managers had direct, actual knowledge that substantial numbers of children in the archdiocese had been sexually abused by substantial numbers of priests." And it concluded that the "widespread abuse of children was due to an institutional acceptance of abuse and a massive and pervasive failure of leadership. . . . They chose to protect the image and reputation of their institution rather than the safety and well-being of the children entrusted to their care" (2002, 25, 73).[2] Such conclusions would have been shocking and explosive in any city in the country. However, this was Boston: the most Catholic of all US cities, in which the number of self-identified Catholics composed more than half of the metropolitan population. As the investigative staff of the *Globe* emphasized, "In no other major American city are Catholics more represented in police precincts, in courtrooms, in boardrooms" (2002, 7).

One reason that the widespread and systematic abuse remained secret for so long had to do with the Church's practice of settling with individual victims who sued the Church. These settlements included confidentiality clauses, or gag orders, thus ensuring that the crimes and the cover-up were never made public. There were also longstanding and unspoken agreements among Boston law enforcement, the plaintiffs' bar who represented the victims, and Church officials not to publicly air the misdeeds of the abusive priests and tarnish the authority of the Church. The extent of the abuse and cover-up only came to light because the *Boston Globe* filed a request to unseal these records with the indictment of Geoghan in 2001. To the great surprise of the archdiocese, the presiding superior court judge, Constance Sweeney, agreed in November of that year that revoking confidentiality was in the public interest and ordered the release of the evidence. Among the many documents that were made public as a result of the court order, none expressed the callous disregard of victims and the tolerance of the crimes more than a note that Cardinal Bernard Law wrote to John Geoghan in 1996, years after his abuse of children was known by the Church. "Yours has been an effective life of ministry, sadly impaired by illness. On behalf of those you have served well, and in my own name, I would like to thank you" (2002, 14).

Confronting the stark characterization of the Attorney General, many Boston-area Catholics reported experiencing a stew of emotions including shock, outrage, sorrow, and bewilderment. Their world was shaken, their trust shattered. Years later, many likened the effects of the abuse crisis to the terrorist attacks of September 11. In the face of the unmooring of their faith and the intense emotions it provoked, they were not sure how to react or what to do. Searching for ways to understand what was happening within their Church, a small group of parishioners of St. John the Evangelist in Wellesley, Massachusetts, organized a series of informal meetings that began in mid-February with several dozen parishioners. The group quickly developed a core leadership, including a doctor who, as a founder of International Physicians for the Prevention of Nuclear War, had shared a Nobel Peace Prize; a well-respected management professor at Boston University; and two parishioners who held master's degrees in divinity from a local Catholic theological seminary. Word spread quickly of these lay gatherings, and soon hundreds were attending these listening sessions from many parishes in the archdiocese. These included future members of St. Erasmus VOTF such as Sister Bridget.

At the early meetings, some who were present shared stories of their own or their family's experiences with abuse at the hands of priests. For many this was the first time they had spoken publicly about the abuse, often noting that up until this point they thought they were the only ones to be victimized this way. Everyone felt betrayed, incredulous that the very people who they thought would protect children were willing to sacrifice them in order to preserve the reputation of the Church. In these early meetings, people saw the Church as they never had before: as secretive, impervious, remote, and uncaring. They were shocked by this terrible knowledge and stung by betrayal, but there was also great expectation and hope. As a columnist for the *Globe* characterized these sessions, "the atmosphere at the Voice of the Faithful meetings resembles a birthing class more than a wake" (*Boston Globe*, April 14, 2002).

The St. John's group prepared a statement for the annual archbishop's convocation in March, which several thousand local Catholics regularly attended. In his address to the assembly, Cardinal Law announced,

I have heard feelings of anger, I have heard feelings of betrayal and that that betrayal is a sense of betrayal by the Church. . . . I have heard you passionately and prayerfully plead for greater openness in the Church, more effective and consistent communication. . . . I have heard calls for greater and more meaningful lay involvement of the laity. . . . And I am going to disappoint you once again by saying that I don't have the answers for you today.

The cardinal emphasized that in using the phrase "We are the Church" during convocations he meant to convey this in an inclusive sense: "It isn't just a throwaway line when I say we are the Church. It's been the lodestar of what spiritually has characterized my life" (*The Pilot*, March 15, 2002, 2SS).[3] "We the Church" was to become a signal phrase of VOTF, but with a very different meaning, asserting legitimate voice and more inclusion in the decision-making of Church affairs.

A representative from the St. John's group took her place in line and, in front of the five hundred gathered, read a carefully prepared statement in which she offered some answers the cardinal lacked. She drew on the cardinal's use of the phrase "We are the Church" to characterize Voice of the Faithful. She began, "We are the Church":

We call ourselves Voice of the Faithful. Voice of the Faithful seeks consensus in order to effectively respond to this scandal threatening our Church. We are sadly aware that pedophilia is a problem not only here but in other cities and countries. The culture of secrecy and abuses of power that produced this crisis must end. The overriding concerns that have emerged from our discussions are the desire to be fully responsive to the victims of pedophilia and their families; and to ensure that appropriate measures are taken to preclude future occurrences; to support clergy of integrity tarnished by this scandal; and to seek correction of the institutional structures of the Catholic Church that resulted in a gravely flawed response to this terrible betrayal of children. (Muller and Kenney 2004, 45)

Six weeks from their initial meeting, the group formally established an organization that many felt would help the Church recover from the damage done by the decades of abuse and cover-up. The group's motto expressed the terms of its engagement: "Keep the faith, change the Church." At one time Voice of the Faithful claimed some 40,000 registrants and 105 affiliates. With this growth the organization established a national office in Boston. Initially the trustees and the office staff heavily reflected the group's Boston origins. Indeed, several St. Erasmus VOTFers regularly volunteered at the national office. However, as the organization expanded in the northeast and beyond there was increasing differentiation and distance between the national office and local chapters, including St. Erasmus, which we explore in chapter 4.

VOTF explicitly casts itself as a broad-based organization in an effort to encompass Catholics of all hues and leanings. It consciously abstained from taking positions on what it considered to be potentially divisive issues, such as the marriage of priests and the ordination of women. "We are mainstream Catholics," the president of the organization was to say later, "What they believe, we believe" (France 2004, 514). In reaching out to the archdiocese as concerned and faithful laity, they anticipated a welcome reception from a hierarchy in crisis, but they were soon disabused of this expectation. In late May, three members of the group sat at a conference table with the second-in-command in the archdiocese, the Vicar General Bishop Edyvean, who was flanked by a young canon lawyer, Mark O'Connell, and received a steely reception.[4] They were quickly shocked to hear stern rebukes by the latter that the group was undermining the leadership of the cardinal, and dismayed to hear the bishop acknowledge that he had taken steps to block the formation of a chapter at another parish. As leader James Muller recounts, "I was astonished that a bishop would act *against* some of the most enthusiastic Catholics in his archdiocese who were acting in compliance with all of the rules of the Church" (Muller and Kenney 2004, 7). The bishop finally allowed that chapters would be permitted to continue to meet on parish grounds but that, as the archdiocese spokesperson later asserted, "it is the diocesan bishop's role to exercise vigilance with regard to the way in which Catholic associations perform the tasks they set for themselves" (*Boston Globe*, May 24, 2002).

Bewilderment shaded to feelings of antagonism over the succeeding months as VOTF leadership realized that the archdiocese framed their organization as adversarial and mutinous. Regardless, chapters continued to proliferate, both in the Boston area and elsewhere on the East Coast. As their numbers swelled the leadership made plans for an ambitious convention on July 21, 2002, at the Hynes Convention Center in Boston, anticipating 4,000 attendees.

For the growing membership this was a signal event. In the St. Erasmus chapter there was sufficient enthusiasm to rent a bus for the many that planned to attend. Sister Bridget remembered the moment they were about to leave when the pastor boarded the bus: "[He] got on the bus and he said, 'I just want to tell you, to encourage you to do what you're doing. I think what you're doing is very important and I want to give you my blessing.'" She likened the convention itself to the spiritual nature of her first trip to the Wellesley meeting: "That was such an event. It was analogous to that wind and fire. This big place with all these people and wonderful presenters. It was dynamite really. And that was a life-giving booster to the whole effort." Despite her initial skepticism about the *Boston Globe*'s motives, Victoria Swingewood, a retired English professor, also recalled her feelings of exhilaration. "I went to the convention, which was just wonderful. It was just amazing. . . . It really was. It was just this feeling of unity."

Arthur Austin, a survivor and vocal critic of the archdiocese, challenged the attendees to march a mile in solidarity with him and other
survivors from the convention center to the Cathedral of the Holy
Cross, the heart of the archdiocese. Immediately after the final Mass
he walked arm in arm with a VOTF leader out of the building and hundreds followed. Florence Anderson recalled, "That was a very pivotal
moment. . . . The survivors, they were just incredible. I mean, they were
crying. They were so emotional. Many of them spoke about how they'd
been coming down [to the cathedral to protest]. And there were always
a few people early on that came down. But it was like having four or five
hundred of us down there to support them. . . . [T]hat was really important. And I think after that, I mean I just couldn't, I just had to be there."

A delegate from the healing and assistance ministry of the archdiocese
had positive initial reactions to the meeting. Barbara Thorp pronounced
after an afternoon workshop on survivors, "This is a great moment of
light. All deeds of the evil shame done by priests and Church representatives [inflicted] great harm to children. . . . As a Church, we must do everything we can to make sure it never happens again" (*The Pilot*, July 26,
2002, 6). The euphoria of the convention and such initially positive re-
marks were quickly countered by the hostility of the archdiocese. The
hierarchy engaged in a campaign against VOTF that Muller termed "a
third scandal" and then-president Jim Post framed as a "declaration of
war" (Muller and Kenney 2004, 224). Reporting on the conference, the
archdiocese's official paper noted that one of the speakers at the convention was a representative of a reformist group started in Germany, We Are
Church, which sought substantial democratic opening of governance. It
headlined a story with "Boston reform movement inspired by dissident
international group" (*The Pilot*, July 26, 2002, 4). In the same issue the
lead editorial was openly critical of VOTF:

The July 20th Voice of the Faithful (VOTF) Conference confirmed our worst fears. Overriding an initial "mainstream" position on Church issues, keynote speakers derided the
hierarchical structure of the Church. . . . To support those who have been abused, to support priests of integrity, and *even* to shape some changes within the Church can, in themselves, be virtuous goals, as long as they are pursued in communion with the Church, and
not with confrontation and division. . . . It is our hope that the ongoing conversations
with the archdiocese will provide opportunity also for them to listen, not only to speak.
Otherwise VOTF will become yet another splinter group. (*The Pilot*, July 26, 2002, 12)

Others loyal to Cardinal Law joined in denouncing the group. Deal
Hudson, the publisher and editor of the influential Catholic magazine

Crisis, characterized VOTF as "simply another group of dissenters, plain and simple," while the prominent conservative scholar Michael Novak accused the organization of being outright secessionists: "The one thing clear is that this new group does not want to be Catholic, as Catholic has been understood by, say, the Councils of Trent, Vatican I, and Vatican II" (*Globe,* August 17, 2002). A prominent local Catholic, who had himself sought to establish an independent group of pastoral councils in response to the sexual abuse crisis, condemned VOTF as counterproductive and obstructionist: "The group has taken an unrepentantly adversarial posture toward bishops in particular and ecclesial authority in general. . . . Unless Voice of the Faithful leadership changes its approach and has a change of heart, the organization will surely be irrelevant to any sort of authentically Catholic reform" (*National Catholic Register,* August 29, 2003, 22). And an archdiocese member loyal to the hierarchy who started an oppositional website called "Faithful Voice" was even more acerbic: "The stuff of schism. The odor of intoxicating power. The acrimonious smell of sulphur. This sheep smells like a wolf."[5]

On October 12, Cardinal Law banned the use of parish facilities by new VOTF chapters, though the several dozen existing chapters were allowed to remain.[6] The archdiocese and the organization sparred over VOTF's establishment of a fund separate from the bishop's annual campaign for Catholic charities. The purpose of the separate fund was to assure donors that no money would be used to offset legal expenses regarding abuse cases.

Law, much to his consternation, was ultimately to lose this battle as the drumbeat for his resignation continued. During the first week of December in 2002, a new trove of archdiocesan documents on the scandal was released. On December 11, VOTF formally called for his resignation. Two days earlier, fifty-eight priests from the Boston Priests' Forum had signed a public letter informing the cardinal that it was necessary for him to step down for healing to begin. "The priests and people of Boston have lost confidence in you as their spiritual leader," they boldly asserted in an unprecedented step by a group of clergy (France 2004, 560). On December 13 Pope John Paul II expressed great gratitude to the cardinal for his service and accepted his resignation. Law was gone from Boston, and VOTF continued to expand its presence.[7]

The Catholics who met in those months after the scandal broke caught a revealing reflection of themselves as lay Catholics. Sitting in St. John's parish hall and later in other church basements and libraries and town halls across the country, sharing stories of abuse and betrayed trust, these Catholics confronted the isolation, silence, and powerlessness of the laity within the Church. Yet almost none of the members of what would become the St. Erasmus chapter of VOTF seriously considered leaving the Church. At the same time, none of them imagined that she would commit herself to a lifetime of activism either.

As they sought a responsive path to the crisis VOTFers, steeped in their faith, relied on some core principles of Catholic social thought. Some of these strands are centuries old, while others are particularly accentuated by the doctrine of Vatican II and inflected by the history of the Church in the US. One key aspect of such thought is *sensus fidei*:

. . . individual believers possess a sense of faith (*sensus fidei*), an inner capacity to discern both religious truth and what is contrary to it. In its more objective dimension, it is expressed as "sense of the faithful" (*sensus fidelium*), which refers to those religious truths upon which, in light of believers' concrete experience of living out their faith, the church as a whole has come to some agreement and about which it cannot err. (Baggett 2008, 233; see also Palacios 2007, 29)

Based in reason through the principles of natural law, as well as biblical teaching, all baptized members of the Church engage in the process of discernment through which they accept responsibility for realizing and enacting the Gospel. As Vatican II emphasized, all People of God play an active role in annunciating and forwarding the faith. The basis for this more particularly is found in a "communitarian personalism". The latter emphasizes the dignity of each human being as "morally free and accountable, and bearing intrinsic rights and duties," while the former is based on core ideas of solidarity among the faithful in which members come to broad corporatist understanding of their shared visions and responsibilities (Pope 2004, 31; Palacios 2007, 44–47; Baggett 2008, 18: Groome 2002, 157).[8]

These guiding principles encourage active interpretation of tradition (Groome 2002, 153). This involves negotiation and reappropriation of tradition as an act of living faith rather than blind obedience (Baggett 2008, 215–16; Groome 2002, 24–26). All of these precepts are harnessed in the service of the Church's social mission, which is the pursuit of social justice and the common good: As the 1971 World Synod of Bishops declared, "'Action on behalf of justice and participation in the transformation of the world fully appear to us as a *constitutive dimension of the preaching of the Gospel*, or, in other words, of the Church's mission for the redemption of the human race and its *liberation from every oppressive situation.*' In other words, working for social justice is integral to living the gospel and to the mission of the Church in the world" (Groome 2002,

213; see also Carmella 2001, 259; Hornsby-Smith 2006, 93). All of these ideas motivate an understanding that "Roman Catholicism is as much a verb as a noun" (Schuck 2013, 252).

In the years since the revelations of sexual abuse, membership in the national VOTF has declined and a number of the original Boston-area chapters have disappeared. Yet one affiliate, St. Erasmus VOTF, persisted for fifteen years. Over the years they have been criticized by fellow Catholics and denounced by the Church hierarchy for their work. They have accepted and spoken frankly about the improbability of changing the Church in their lifetimes. They have weathered internal conflict and even tragedy. How, then, have they sustained their activism and embraced their identities as activists in the face of dwindling participation, a receding sense of success, leadership succession, papal transitions, and unending waves of newly discovered scandals?

In the following pages we focus on the dynamics of collective identity, but this analysis also is intended to address how engagement in activism is often a phenomenological process, a shift from the dominant thinking in social movement research.

St. Erasmus VOTF

The small group commemorating the eleventh anniversary of the revelations of abuse had been meeting in the basement of St. Erasmus parish every Monday night since they formed their own affiliate a few short months after the scandal broke. Much as was the case with St. John's in Wellesley, the St. Erasmus group was born of an initial series of listening sessions with the encouragement of the current pastor. Those who attended these meetings remember them as being crowded and boisterous, with well over one hundred people. As Grace Heffernan recalled, "Basically people came and they vented. And people ranted and cried and, you know, and said what an awful thing it was. . . . And you would hear people who had taught your kids in religious education saying 'I hate this Church. Look what it's doing.' And, you know, just terribly, terribly raw feelings." Joe Fitch recalled that after some initial uncertainty the pastor at St. Erasmus encouraged the attendees to affiliate: "I was forever grateful. He seemed to really care that this was happening . . . and said, 'Please have a Voice of the Faithful chapter here.'" Indeed, after a few listening sessions, the group became a VOTF affiliate. People who had participated in listening sessions at other parishes, hearing of the newly formed chapter at St. Erasmus, migrated to the group. As Phil

Harper, a former priest, recalled, "I didn't know anybody there. . . . I just walked in off the street." He was struck by how the members of the group were so deeply committed to the Church: "[T]hey'd go around the group and say, 'How many people are readers of the Liturgy?' and other questions concerning their parish participation. And so you know, forty hands would go up. 'How many people teach CCD?' And thirty hands would go up. 'And how many people are Eucharistic Ministers?' Eighty hands would go up. So you'd see, visually, these 'dissidents' involved in their parishes."

Without exception St. Erasmus VOTFers attribute both the rapid formation of the chapter and its remarkable endurance to the dynamism of one member, Peter Hall, who quickly assumed a kind of pastoral leadership: coordinating but never commanding, fostering and facilitating members' passions and efforts. In his forties, Peter was among the youngest members of St. Erasmus VOTF. A lawyer with a major firm in Boston, Peter was a longtime member of the parish, but not a vocal participant. Other members remembered him as an unassuming parishioner in the pews who they recognized by sight, but with whom they had never spoken. Without any formal decision by the group, Peter emerged as a powerful presence and de facto leader. From the start Peter urged the group to commit to weekly Monday meetings. He was adamant that less regular meetings would erode their commitment and eventually lead to the demise of the group.

In this early period, at least one meeting a month was devoted to working groups based on the three planks established at St. John's. Each working group focused on developing specific undertakings with near-term goals. Florence Anderson recalled the frenetic energy of these sessions: "There was so much going on and there were so many things to do. You know everybody's sectioned off in different groups. And you wanted to be part of every group." Fairly quickly members coalesced around one of the three planks and informal principles emerged for each working group. Shirley Tropea, who strongly identified with the structural change working group, remembered how many concerns bubbled up in the open discussions:

At our first meeting of structural change at St. Erasmus we had so many people that we took not only that downstairs room [the church basement hall], we went up into the rooms where they have CCD classes. . . . [I said,] "Now you're going to tell me what your grievances are . . ." And they're telling me and I'm writing them down. We must have had a hundred different things. . . . Celibacy was always there at the top of the list. Women priests. . . . It just brought out everything.

Eventually, in collaboration with other chapters, St. Erasmus whittled down the unwieldy list of issues to focus on more effective communication between the laity and the hierarchy. The structural change group set out to gain positions on the local parish council and engage in outreach to figures in the archdiocese in order to start productive dialogue.

At the same time that the structural change group was defining core goals, the group working on supporting survivors pursued its own agenda: creating a fundraising scheme to raise money for survivors to attend national conferences sponsored by Survivors Network of those Abused by Priests (SNAP), developing ties with survivors and their allies, and bringing survivors to meetings where they could tell their stories of abuse to an audience who would listen attentively and sympathetically. Members drawn to the third working group, supporting priests of integrity, developed and conducted a survey of diocesan priests[9] to assess their concerns and needs. The leaders of each working group also represented the chapter in the regional- and national-level working groups. Since their faith was the foundation of their decision to remain within the Church, the chapter also engaged in faith-sharing exercises to deepen their spirituality.

Over the years, the size of St. Erasmus VOTF has varied depending on the program, the weather, or the time of the year. When we began attending in 2007, the group attracted forty or fifty people on a weekly basis. These days, a much smaller group of about twenty highly committed members meets regularly, although that number may swell occasionally for an anniversary or a well-known speaker. The remaining regulars schedule events, maintain distribution lists, keep abreast of national VOTF activities, and run the weekly meetings. Although they made a commitment to meet every Monday evening—what a number of them have called their "Sabbath"—that commitment too has been relaxed. They now take off the summer as well as the dark weeks in winter. While the group is smaller, it has become more committed to its mission—a mission that has evolved to become more ambitious over time.

One of us dropped in on a sparsely attended planning session as part of our ongoing efforts to remain in touch with the group several years after our intensive fieldwork ended. The meeting's agenda was to map out programming for the spring and earlier summer. However, the discussion quickly became more expansive as these veteran members raised fundamental questions about the course of their activities and future possibilities. Grace observed that more than ten years on, members were older and perhaps couldn't maintain the effort involved in weekly meetings. She also reflected that "we have all morphed into something over the last twelve years." She then followed up with a rhetorical question about Francis I, the newly named pope who had succeeded the more conservative Pope Benedict XVI: "Are we all done now that [Pope] Francis is here? I think not."

These musings led to a dialogue on fundamental group concerns. Thomas McNally suggested that they might have a discussion of how members understood the group's collective identity, given that its members still maintained diverse understandings of its mission and focus. Phil Harper pitched in that this also raised the question of the group's direction, and a little later observed that he had come to realize that the group's project was "not a five- or ten-year thing, but a fifty-year thing." The discussion moved into consideration of a "strategy audit" list that Grace had been given by a worker in the national office, which asked a series of prospective questions so that groups could map out a sense of the future. As they responded to the list Phil reflected, "I guess I'm not sure what success looks like." A little while later Thomas responded that success should be measured as sustainability, and that if the chapter existed fifty years from now it would be a success. "Maybe," he ruminated, "existing is enough," and he offered the persistence of the US feminist movement as an example of what they might aspire toward. The conversation meandered. Members noted that some of the early participants had "flamed out" or left because of ideological disagreements. They reminisced about Peter's early leadership, noted the commitment and congeniality of continuing members, considered the ascendance of Pope Francis, and worried a bit about the lack of younger members. After ninety minutes they participated in the ritual closing prayer, without any conclusions about the meaning of success or agreement regarding future direction, but with a clear understanding that they would return the following week.

At both the national and local level, VOTF has faced enormous obstacles in pursuing its goals of reform. The Catholic Church is one of the most powerful, richest, and largest organizations in the world, making its reform by a relatively small group of inexperienced activists improbable. Moreover, all of the St. Erasmus VOTFers had grown up as faithful Catholics and continue to stake much of their personal identity on that faith. In pursuing change, they thus had to overcome their own subjective reluctance to become challengers, as well as the hostility they encountered from the Church hierarchy and, in some cases, from other Catholics.

Looking back over the life of VOTF as a national organization, political scientist Peter McDonough dismissed their efforts, concluding that

"Voice of the Faithful looked like a social movement in the sense that Pluto was thought to be a planet. . . . Claims of moral victory, of having changed the conversation, rang hollow" (2013, 163). McDonough's summary judgment overlooks much of the meaningful work they accomplished over the years. St. Erasmus VOTF has constituted itself as the "conscience of the Church," received recognition and affirmation from some who initially were skeptical of their efforts, and, perhaps most importantly, members have begun to live the faith that they initially envisioned. Indeed, a central argument of this book is that this dismal assessment of VOTF's success or impact indicates more a failure of imagination than a failure of the group. The persistence of VOTF in the face of the hurdles they encountered challenges us to enlarge our sense of what constitutes activism and agency and to reconsider how we define social movement "success." We will return to this matter of persistence at the end of this analysis, after pursuing a detailed analysis of the collective identity process.

What Is a Social Movement?

While social scientists offer abundant definitions of the term *social movement*, they rarely, if ever, interrogate the metaphorical purchase of the word *movement* in the phrase; none specify what it is that moves or, perhaps, what it is that is being moved. Is it that people are moved to join or act (suggesting a focus on mobilization and the construction of grievances)? Or does the term signify change: to move society toward some desirable end (implying an instrumental rationality)? While the word does reference all of these, its meaning nonetheless often remains tacit. We propose—in the semiotic space that has been left vacant—to explore the metaphor of movement for purposes of clarifying our theoretical assumptions and empirical aims.

Movement, as Anna Lowenhaupt Tsing (2005) reminds us, does not occur without friction. Movement in both the literal and figurative sense occurs, in other words, only with engagement and resistance— out of the "sticky materiality of practical encounters" (1). Similarly, Nina Eliasoph (1998) employs Erving Goffman's metaphor of "footing" to understand how people "make a path by walking it, the ways ideas mingle and interact." Footing, Eliasoph writes, is the "[C]onstant, unspoken process of assessing the grounds for interaction. Are there stairs here? Loose gravel? Ice? To walk we have to assess the footing. Talking is the same: are we talking to make conversation, to accomplish a task?

To show off?" (21) More fundamentally, in order to walk—that is, to move—there has to be gravel, or ice, or stairs, or something with which we can have a sticky (or slippery) encounter. The resistance the ground offers and our adaptation to it creates traction. The distance, direction, and velocity of a "movement" is both enabled and constrained by the character of these encounters. As Kathleen Blee (2012) suggests, this stickiness can create a path dependent process for contention, though it is never wholly determinative.

Thus, social "movement" not only refers to that which is moved (activists or society) but also to the "on-the-ground" engagements: encounters with others (activists, allies, and opponents), as well as encounters with the past, present, and future. Our project aims to examine the friction and the footing—the sticky materiality of practical encounters of one affiliate of Voice of the Faithful. Our key focus is on these ongoing and on-the-ground encounters through which challengers create, enact, and transform their collective identities.

Research on social movements often focuses on critical phases in the life span of a movement: mobilization (how participants are recruited to a cause), repertoires of contention (how movements engage with opponents in seeking change), and outcomes (how movements end or decline as well as the transformations they produce). In this book we adopt a different approach and engage a different set of questions relating to collective efforts to bring about social change. Rather than focus on the beginning, middle, and end of movements, we examine the emergent nature of collective action and collective actors. This book is not about strategies of institutional change as much as it is about the processes through which activists become change seekers. This is a story of identities under stress and the identity work that comes to constitute their activism. Therefore, rather than ask how participants are recruited, we ask how movement participants continually and collectively reconstitute themselves and their cause. How do they reconcile and refashion their identities as challengers with their constellation of other identities as citizens, family members, or loyal Catholics? Rather than assess movement strategies and tactics, we explore the ongoing interpretive and narrative work that activists engage in as they navigate pasts, presents, and futures with a changing cast of characters and plot lines.

Our research grows out of an emergentist approach toward social movements advocated by Kathleen Blee (2012, 2013) through which we see challenging groups as always in process. The shared meanings through which activism is pursued are never finalized, and the intertwining of group culture and action cannot be reduced to rational action.

Activist repertoires are winnowed early on by decisions of nascent groups, but they remain contingent and subject to significant transformations.

By adopting an emergentist approach, we are not entirely forfeiting larger questions about mobilization, repertoires, or efficacy; we are reframing these dynamics to capture their processual (and phenomenological) character. Since action is always local, the processes of mobilization, the selection of repertoires, and the outcome of any movement—as well as everything that occurs between those critical moments—always happen in the context of the particular lives, relationships, and interactions that constitute the here and now.

In attempting to change the Church, the aim of VOTF parallels that of many change seekers whose efforts are overwhelmed by the economic resources, political power, and scale of the institutions they seek to change. In a world where the objects of change seekers are elusive and mobile, and where the exercise of power is remote in time and place, it is all the more necessary to reimagine the possibilities and limitations of challenge. In the case of the Church crisis and the VOTF response, expectations of obedience, deference to hierarchy, presumptions of ecclesiastic immunity, and distrust of secular law collided with liberal and reformist commitments to the individual conscience, liberty, and democracy. Caught between their loyalty to the Church and their sense of being empowered citizens, VOTF members reimagined their Church and their role in it. In the process, they reimagined themselves as Catholics. Theirs then is an all-too-familiar story about identities under stress, about institutional betrayal and the restoration of trust, about commitment and the meaning of justice.

The predicament that VOTF faced is particularly salient for "challengers within," that is, groups working for change within an organization of which they are members. Work on such groups has typically focused on "institutional activists" or "insiders" within the state who not only abet but are an active force in transformational change (Banaszak 2010; Katzenstein 1998; Pettinicchio 2012; Santoro and McGuire 1997). Much of this research focuses on the role of feminists inside state institutions. Here we are more interested in people who belong to an institution but do not have sanctioned authority within it. The Church was central to the lives of St. Erasmus VOTFers, but, as they discovered, their voices were not central to the workings of the archdiocese. If, as these studies suggest, challenges are increasingly occurring within institutions, then we need to focus on how those who are inside but not "insiders" pursue transformation in ways large and small.

In *Democracy in the Making*, Blee studies what she describes as "tiny and short-lived" activist groups. She recognizes that the impact of such groups is often underestimated insofar as the work they do is ontological and prefigurative. Blee, citing Robin D. G. Kelley, notes that these fragile groups "do what great poetry always does: transport us to another place, compel us to relive horrors, and, more importantly, enable us to imagine a new society" (2012, 3). This is a story of how St. Erasmus VOTFers responded to the crisis and in so doing not only sought to aid survivors, support priests of integrity, and push for structural change, but also attempted to change fundamental understandings of being Catholic.

In the next chapter, we lay out our theoretical perspective on collective identity and the emergentist approach behind it. We offer a model of collective identity conceived of as having three axes. One axis references a group's existence across time. A second axis maps a group's relationships with those outside of the group, what we call the external relational axis. Finally, group identity emerges out of the relationships among members, or internal relational axis. Our focus is on how groups are constantly negotiating identity as they move along these three axes. The push and pull of these three axes create the sense of an entity with some sense of itself, and, further that this sense is critical to action. Chapters 2, 3, and 4 take up each axis in our collective identity perspective: the temporal, the external-relational, and the internal-relational. While we acknowledge that many of our examples crosscut these axes, we analytically separate them to examine how each contributes to the process of identity work. We end by considering the insights this case offers for our understanding of the process of collective identity more generally in the study of social movements and collective action.

ONE

Collective Identity and Narrative Practice

As the sexual abuse scandal unfolded, the members of St. Erasmus VOTF faced a number of distressing questions and dilemmas. In deciding how to respond to the crisis, long-standing norms of obedience and deference to the Church collided with their outrage, conscience, and sense of injustice. How could they continue to be faithful and critical of the Church hierarchy? How could they chart a change-seeking course and remain committed to the traditions of the Church? In addressing these questions, the members of St. Erasmus VOTF collectively reconstructed themselves and their cause not only in their initial response to the crisis, but in the years since. As change seekers working within an institution—what we have called "challengers within"—they were required to reconcile and refashion their identities as faithful Catholics with their project of challenging and changing the Church. Our analysis follows these unfolding identity processes and is predicated on a shift in some long-standing presuppositions about collective action and collective identity.

According to the dominant model of social movements, the work of challenging groups has an underlying instrumental or strategic logic. This strategic view of social movements shapes how we envision the dynamics of collective challenge. Within this model, groups perceive inequity and injustice, define shared grievances, and adopt an oppositional identity and politics. This politics establishes goals that give purpose and direction to contention, including mobilization, framing, and contentious action itself. In this perspective, groups coalesce around their purposes and end goals at a relatively early stage, and these serve as the basis for the adoption of strategies and tactics during the course of contention. As Amin Ghaziani observes in his critique of this model, strategies "specify the end goals of collective action along with the means for obtaining them" (2008, 18).

Much scholarship on social movement culture and identity politics also relies on some version of this model. Challengers are thought to construct their collective identities to best secure their goals. Movement entrepreneurs strategically engage in culture work such as framing both to recruit others to join the group and to remind and reassure fellow activists to stay on track. The dominant framework, thus, focuses on an underlying and animating purpose for action that signposts the road between a group's self-realization and the realization of their goals.

We offer an alternative perspective in which challengers forge a path to pursue change as much as they follow one. Suspending the assumptions in the dominant model concerning purposes and goals, we examine the emergent nature of collective action and collective actors. We emphasize the reflexivity of activists and how they routinely engage in action and conjure identities as they challenge authority. Groups are self-referential projects, continually reshaping themselves in relation to their prior affiliations, the outcome of previous action, the responses of others, and their prospects for the proximate and distant future.[1] We approach collective challenge as an ongoing adaptive process in which activists map itineraries as they move, and we see our framework as complementary to the dominant model.

Following Kathleen Blee's innovative work, we call this orientation an emergentist perspective, one that is necessarily keyed to micro processes of social action. Blee uses the term *emergent* to examine "how collective properties of activist groups emerge from and shape individual action, as well as how the actions of individual members sustain or resist this process" (2013, 660). Activism, she writes, is "a process, ever being made" (2012, 4). Our approach similarly focuses on the relational and dynamic nature of social movements.

Instead of focusing on the immanent logic of strategic goals embedded in the dominant model, we conceptualize action in terms of projects. Projects are the broadly imagined transformed futures animated by stories. They differ from goals in that their specifics are emergent in the flow of action. "Ends and means develop conterminously within contexts that are themselves ever changing and thus always subject to reevaluation and reconstruction" (Emirbayer and Mische 1998, 966).

Activists' aspirations are partly formed in the process of creating paths of redress; as they move along this course their sense of who they are and what they are doing evolves. This does not mean that change groups are rudderless, but that their shared horizons have multiple and varying foci and are regularly reformulated in the flow of their shared histories, experiences of the present, and projections of the future. In other words, while actors do pursue collective goods, such goods can be formulated in situ and are dynamic ways of "being in the world."

The VOTF project can be summed up in their unofficial motto, "Keep the Faith, Change the Church." The specifics of these aspirations, and how to pursue them, emerged in the flow of action over time and took turns that were unimagined when the motto was coined. They materialized as temporally specific goals responsive to changing contexts. For example, as we detail in the analysis below, St. Erasmus VOTFers came to an understanding that fulfilling these aspirations involved a collective and self-transformation not envisioned in the early stages of the group.

Because groups pursue multiple goals in a project, they are coordinating different senses of the past, present, and future within any given situation. Thus, in any particular context, groups find themselves in a web of collectively imagined time spans, and continued action involves successfully negotiating within these various horizons. "Next" is always keyed to evolving temporal orientations. In Mead's terms, "Durations are a continual sliding of presents into each other." Planning action involves simultaneously locating ourselves in the past and future through a construction of the "future perfect tense" of lived experience (1934, 28).

The persistence of St. Erasmus VOTF is due, in part, to its capacity to move within this web of activities using multiple conceptions of the flow of time. At first, the revelations of the scandal and cover-up produce a crisis of meaning in the present. The experience of crisis alters our sense of time passing. In the midst of such a crisis, time seizes up, encapsulating us in what can feel like an unbearable present fraught with ambiguity. Crisis thus disables our ability to project, to plan, to imagine a future. Paradoxically, while a crisis impedes our ability to plan, it also intensifies our motivation to act. The members of St. Erasmus VOTF, despite their reluctance to get involved or challenge the Church, felt compelled to do something.

This long process of discovering their "own possibilities of being" was present from the beginning—even while they were supporting priests, assisting survivors, and trying to reform Church structures. It was there in the early "listening sessions," where many heard for the first time the distressing and painful stories of other Catholics whom they had silently kneeled next to in Mass for years. It was there as they boarded the bus that would take them to the national VOTF convention at the Hynes Auditorium in Boston only months after the scandal broke. It was there as they congregated in front of churches and cathedrals bearing signs with the childhood pictures of victims. It was present every Monday night in the basement of St. Erasmus as they sang "Amazing Grace," listened to invited speakers, and shared brownies and punch. Although "becoming" was not their only project, it is what we call a "constitutive" project. As they acquired a sense of their own spiritual and social identity, they acted differently. "Becoming" entailed reclaiming their past and reimaging their future. Indeed, as they raised money to assist survivors, organized picnics and panels to support priests, and worked to change the governance structure of parishes and dioceses, they were constituting themselves as simultaneously faithful Catholics and challengers within.

As we have observed, early group decisions have a formative and enduring influence on the makeup, sense of purpose, and dynamics of a challenging group. However, even though a group proceeds along an increasingly familiar path, critical conjunctures—unanticipated events, collective reflections, and altering group dynamics—can disturb the group's sense of purpose and identity and produce unexpected changes in the direction that groups travel. In a signal illustration, Blee examines how a local animal rights group radically changed its course of action. The Animal Liberation League had envisioned themselves as a local group of activists who brought attention to the rights of animals through an eclectic mix of nonconfrontational public actions. However, a campaign to stop the serving of foie gras at area restaurants drastically transformed their sense of purpose within a national animal rights movement. Their orientation shifted from the present to a more distant future where animal abuse would be eliminated. Most significantly, they began imagining themselves as rights warriors, confronting restaurateurs in order to eradicate commercial animal farming. Their increasingly antagonistic actions were invested with emotion and passion. The Animal Liberation League "recomposed itself" based on "a complex mixture of changing realities, its unfolding interpretations of its context, its theories of political action, and its sense of collective competence and efficacy" (2012, 50).

Like Blee, we also theorize challenging groups as experiencing traction and resistance as they encounter the unfolding of historical, situational, and relational realities. Our aim is to explore how a challenging group regularly revisits and imagines its shared understandings of identity and purpose, and at specific junctures significantly reimagines them. As groups confront power and constraint, as well as reflexively narrate their activities, they not only look at the past, but also envision alternative futures projecting "themselves into their own possibilities of being" (Emirbayer and Mische 1998, 986). Such projections of the possible significantly involve the dynamics of collective identity.

Rethinking Collective Identity

There is a crucial link between agency and identity, between what a group believes itself to be and what it does. Holland et al. observe that "Identities are a key means through which people care about and care for what is going on around them. They are important bases from which people create new activities, new worlds, and new ways of being" (1998, 4). For this reason, collective identity is implicated in virtually every aspect of activism. By developing an identity, challengers share a perception of "we-ness"; establish a sense of boundedness; achieve cognitive, moral, and affective solidarity; and recognize common fate, cause, and agency. Collective identity is also context-dependent, keyed to audience, organizational fields, and the larger external environment.

Identity politics involves claiming authorship over, setting boundaries for, and valorizing collective identity. There is an emphasis in the literature on how challengers strategically deploy collective identity to pursue power and resources (Bernstein 2005, 48). Identity can be deployed for critique, confronting "the values, categories, and practices of the dominant culture," or for education, challenging "the dominant culture's perception of the minority or . . . used strategically to gain legitimacy by playing on uncontroversial themes" (Bernstein 2008, 281). Thus, activists can either foreground sameness or difference—engaging in celebration or suppression of collective identities—depending on the situational logic of the political engagement.

In concentrating on the cognitive and instrumental dimensions of identity work, the identity politics literature runs the risk of reifying identity and neglecting its processual, dilemmic, and dialogic dimensions. As Alberto Melucci, among others, has noted, collective identity "must be conceived as a process because it is constructed and negotiated through repeated activation of the relationships that link individuals (or groups)" (1995, 44).[2] In their critique of the collective identity literature, Rogers Brubaker and Frederick Cooper agree, arguing that even while the analytic category of collective identity is defined as a contingent process, entailments of essentialism are secreted into the concept. Scholars tend to lapse into what Brubaker and Cooper call the "category of practice," or folk category of collective identity, as an abiding thing. "Even in its constructivist guise," they write, "the language of 'identity' disposes us to think in terms of bounded groupness. . . . Identity is already 'there,' as something that individuals and groups 'have.' . . . Even constructivist language tends therefore to objectify 'identity,' to treat it as a 'thing,' albeit a malleable one, that people 'have,' 'forge,' and construct" (2000, 27).

Their assumption is that as an analytic concept identity cannot be both essential and emergent, abiding and contingent, an entity and a process. For this reason, Brubaker and Cooper recommend abandoning the concept altogether. By contrast, we argue that the concept of collective identity is not vexed by these contradictions between sameness and difference, or fluidity and permanence, as much as it encompasses them. In their effort to avoid reproducing the "folk category"—and its reifying essentialist tendencies—Brubaker and Cooper dismiss it as "wrong." But what if the folk category (the sense of collective identity as abiding and core) is what the analytic category (identity as process and emergent) needs to explain? In other words, if we take seriously the phenomeno-logical experience of identity as more or less stable and essential, rather than simply dismiss it, we must consider how that experience emerges and is sustained. Furthermore, we must consider why it is significant, particularly for collective action.

We suggest that both dimensions can be involved, that people move through social lives with deep investments in collective identities but that these are the contingent outcomes of ongoing action. In this sense the debate as to whether identity is a product or a process is miscon-ceived (Flesher Fominaya 2010a, 2010b; Snow 2001). Identity is an emergent process that must also have an epiphenomenal stability to it, an imagined and acted-upon concreteness in the moment as actors ne-gotiate its dilemmas. As Giddens (1984) suggests, identity is the process of keeping a story of self going. Such activity, he argues, provides us with an essential ontological security necessary to navigate the provisional nature of ongoing action.[3] Of course, claiming that identity is a process obliges us to consider what mechanisms animate the process. By what logic does it unfold? And, just as important, if identity is not stable and "already there in some form," how does it come to appear, or even feel, to be so? How, in other words, does a process that is constantly unfold-ing appear more or less unchangeable and even essential?

In the chapters that follow, we trace the ways in which individual and group identities of St. Erasmus VOTF changed, and what events and processes accounted for the nature and direction of these changes. At the heart of the process, we argue, is the internally contradictory nature of identity itself. Rather than a singular, stable, and holistic essence, identity is work. It is work because it is often in trouble.

Identity Trouble

"If we want things to stay as they are, things will have to change."
GIUSEPPE TOMASI DI LAMPEDUSA, *THE LEOPARD*

The process of creating, experiencing, and sustaining collective identity (what we call identity work for short) involves three analytically distinct dimensions: the temporal, the external relational, and the internal relational.[4] Each of these falls along an axis that marks sameness or difference. The temporal dimension represents a group's meaningful construction of their situation across time. With regard to the temporal dimension, groups generally strive to achieve a sense of continuity with the past and the future. Of course, continuity does not mean constancy: people and groups change. But in the face of such change, actors must reasonably account for the transformation. Continuity is thus constructed reflexively by the actors through the selective retrieval of memories and the reinterpretation of events such that what has been experienced as chaotic and disruptive seems to unfold in a meaningful way. Because events and experiences are always in flux, identity work necessarily entails an ongoing reconstruction of continuity. But the reflexive interpretation of our past (and future) becomes particularly problematic when emergent events challenge the typical schema for interpretation, thus disrupting the identification of oneself in the flow of time. In the case of groups, a problematic moment appears at that point at which there is no past, at the moment of the group's conception, so to speak. Challengers then find themselves at a point along this temporal axis away from continuity toward discontinuity, jeopardizing ontological security and undermining the grounds for agentic action. In the face of such challenges, continuity must be actively reconfigured in order to repair or, in the case of newly formed groups, to establish identity anew.

Groups often construct origin stories as a way of meaningfully accounting for the emergence of the group by deliberately cleaving it from the past and attributing cause to some external events.[5] Lynn Owens argues that what he terms "origin stories" provide essential narratives for delineating the collective identity of a challenging group, its moral purpose, and an emplotment for future action (2008, 44–45). He also notes that activists revisit these narratives in the unfolding of contention. In the case of VOTF, the revelations of scandal and cover-up presented such a challenge to the individual members' identities as faithful Catholics (and to their belief in a good Church), a basis for their ontological security. At the same time, it offered an opportunity for the development of an emerging—and seemingly discontinuous—identity as challengers. As Owens (2008) and Francesca Polletta (2006) argue, and as we demonstrate with VOTF, origin stories initially deny the agency of the group, shifting the focus to forces beyond their immediate control. This is one of the reasons why origin stories can make action compelling.

The denial of agency that characterizes origin stories, however, poses a problem for the long-term existence of the group. In order for the group to persist, the collective understanding of agency must be reactivated. For this to occur, successor stories must be told. Through such stories challengers construct a narrative understanding of agentic "we-ness."

Collective identity is also constituted through differentiation from and identification with others outside of the group. We refer to this dimension of identity as the external relational axis. Many scholars have emphasized the construction of boundaries in order to define a group as different and separate from nonmembers. This emphasis on the marking of boundaries overlooks the ways in which emergent groups come to understand and present themselves as similar to others with whom they interact, including opponents, allies, and other audiences. In other words, groups move along this axis of sameness and difference in relation to a variety of external constituencies, and it is partly this movement that comes to constitute their identity.

This is particularly germane for challengers within.[6] In the case of VOTF, a great deal of the micromobilization involved boundary-spanning or boundary-dissolving efforts. For instance, in seeking to be recognized and treated as "adult baptized Catholics," responsible Church members who can assist in its continued well-being, they were trying to diminish the traditional and unquestioned distinction between clergy and laity. On another front, VOTF worked to establish themselves as mainstream Catholics, thus bridging the boundary that others were drawing by calling them troublemakers and dissidents. Attention to this axis of variation reveals that group boundaries, particularly for challengers within, are multiple, pliable, and porous.[7] The capacity of boundaries to endow identity may lie less in how they separate and differentiate than in how they are continually reconfigured in the ongoing processes of challenge.

The third axis of variation that constitutes identity refers to relationships among members, what we are calling the "internal relational dimension." Again, where much scholarship in collective identity has rightly focused on the development of a sense of "we-ness," emphasizing the sameness end of this axis, we find that identity also emerges out of internal differences and conflicts.[8] Rather than homogeneity, groups seek internal relational coherence. The goal is not that everyone within the group thinks the same or believes the same, but that the "various activities, thoughts, feelings fit together into some more or less coherent whole" (Hewitt 1989, 153). Indeed, in many cases the integrity of the whole lies in its capacity to contain rather than eliminate the differences and conflicts that occur among members. George Herbert Mead (1934) used the phrase "parliament of selves" to describe the multiplicity of individual identity; collective identity similarly arises out of the integration of a diverse and sometimes conflicting membership.

Each of these three dimensions, as well as the relations among them, is dialogic and dilemmic. Dialogically, identity is an ongoing process, referenced to the past, present, and future in interaction with those inside and outside of the group. By dilemmic, we mean that the incompleteness, tensions, and contradictions of identity are internal to the thing itself. Identity work becomes consciously salient to challenging groups when its dilemmic and tensile aspects appear problematic in the flow of action.

The project of being faithful Catholics exemplifies the dilemmic nature of identity as illustrated in figure 1 below.

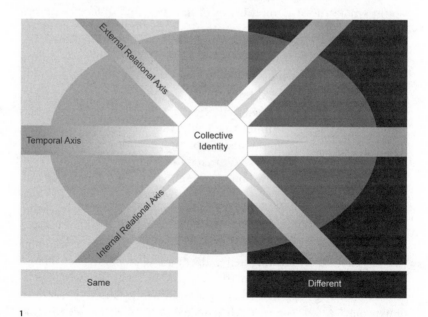

1

Over several years, we observed the ways St. Erasmus VOTF narrated and enacted connection with their pasts and, at the same time, marked attenuation and even rupture (temporality axis). We saw them identify *with*, not simply differentiate *from*, outsiders—including other Catholics not involved in the group, local clergy, hierarchy, and survivors of priest abuse (external relational axis). We observed them participating in practices that fostered identification with one another, constructing "we-ness." But we also saw internal differences drawn and conflicts enacted and accepted (internal relational axis). At times, depending on exigencies, opportunities, and constraints, one of these dimensions became more salient—or more "troublesome"—thus requiring more and different kinds of identity work.

In short, the semblance of a stable, distinctive, and coherent collective identity—the felt "we-ness" that is the phenomenological basis of identity—emerged out of their ongoing work to manage these tensions. Moreover, it is the countervailing pull between these various dimensions, between now–then, sameness–difference, us–them, that provides identity with a tautness, or a tensile stability, that creates the sense of coherence and continuity: that very "thingness" that is belied by the project of identity. These internal tensions also ensure that the process of identity never ends, why it is and must remain a postulate. In other words, were a group to slide entirely to one endpoint or the other, it would precipitate an identity crisis of sorts, a kind of collective collapse. To be totally continuous (or discontinuous) with a past, to be entirely alike (or completely unlike) others, and to have a completely homogeneous (or completely heterogeneous) membership would render a group unidentifiable. Collective identity emerges out of the gaps, fragmentations, and contradictions that occur as we move along these various axes.

Narrative and Identity Work

What does such identity work entail? As we have noted above, a critical piece of it consists of actors telling stories to themselves and to others. According to Hunt, Benford, and Snow, "collective identities are talked into existence" (1994, 45). Moreover, as Arthur Frank observes, "stories and social movements have a natural affinity because stories move people, in the sense of both generating emotions and creating agitation that shifts people's position" (2010, 133).[9] They provide a sense of placement and movement along each axis. One reason narrative is so tightly bound to identity work is that it is capable of "sensibly accounting for" what might appear to be shifting—or even contradictory—temporal and relational boundaries.[10] Storytelling is particularly central to both initial mobilization and the maintenance of contention because it provides emplotment, tying the past, present, and future together in a coherent explanation.

Movement lies at the heart of story. Narratives are defined by the unfolding of events, conflict, and resolution.[11] Margaret Somers, for example, claims that "people construct identities (however multiple and changing) by locating themselves or being located within a repertoire of emplotted stories" (1994, 614). She argues that people produce ontological narratives from a limited stock of available stories to anchor a sense of being and becoming in the world (1992, 603).[12] Narratives are bundles of practices through which emplotments are enacted. They are storied acts. In addition to more conventional stories that are told (and retold), collective identity work also takes the form of what Kenneth Gergen calls "lived narratives" or "forms of social interchange that we understand or index in narrative terms" (2005, 112).[13]

Francesca Polletta (2006) artfully demonstrates this process in her narrative analysis of the Greensboro lunch counter sit-ins. After the initial sit-in, activists offered a narrative of how the protest was the result of "spontaneous combustion," what we have termed an origin story. This story was silent on the process of mobilization, but provided rich imaginings of a people so burdened that they were compelled to act— and in the account this combustion was the spark for a much larger fire that swept out of Greensboro. Polletta emphasizes that this narrative work allowed the students to shed an externally imposed identity as apathetic, break with a more moderate politics of adults, and identify an unstoppable moral force that moved toward wide horizons.

Narrative theorists argue that institutional embeddedness provides actors with such stories or scripts and organizational forms for collective action. They emphasize that institutions provide cultural models and repertoires of practices that both enable and constrain. Many analyses of the Civil Rights movement have emphasized how narratives in the black church provided a template for lived narratives of protest. St. Erasmus VOTFers frequently referenced continuity with Vatican II as they asserted the role of their voice in Church governance. In this sense embeddedness provides ongoing narratives of both autobiography and collective identity.[14] Institutional participation supplies durable stories of a life course and community involvement, but since such accounts are open-ended, they offer "the invitation to a sequel, the necessity of a future" (Merleau-Ponty quoted in Crossley 2004, 98). Institutions can provide highly salient bases for narrative identity through which ongoing processes of self and community attachment unfold. Producing their collective identity as faithful Catholics, St. Erasmus VOTFers relationally referenced this narrative of tradition as they moved within orientations to the past, present, and future.

In part they did so through ritualized practices, and we see a tie between narrative and ritual. As Grace Yukich suggests, "People share identity not only through the use of words but also in concrete practices that embody their stories. These deeper-than-words rituals and practices can be more powerful in constructing identity than mere words" (2010, 174).[15] Ritual is a form of lived narrative, and both "give meaning to our world in part by linking the past to the present and the present to the future," providing ongoing temporality to group action (Kertzer 1988, 9–10). Rituals are formalized and iterative stories that anchor actors within institutional histories. Such use of ritual has been noted by scholars who have analyzed the practices of other Catholic activist groups (Spickard 2005; Summers Effler 2010). For the St. Erasmus VOTFers, as challengers within, the appropriation of institutional rituals that we discuss in later chapters became a significant means by which they could negotiate their position along the three axes of identity. Through rituals, they located themselves in flows of time, navigating their position on the axis of self and other, and crafted a means by which internal multiplicity could be expressed through unity.

A final important aspect of the narrative process is the way in which it constructs bounded ambiguity. Stories provide a sense of directionality but are not completely prescriptive, allowing people to read themselves into collective identity and action.[16] This ambiguity is contained both by the plot lines available to challengers given their institutional contexts and by the emplotment of stories used to initially organize collective identities and mobilization. When storytelling is successful this ambiguity is also important, we suggest, for cognitively and emotionally navigating the dilemmas, contradictions, and ambivalences of contention, such as those of collective identity which we noted earlier. Challengers can draw on stories to recognize and manage competing identities, or to sublimate the importance of one or more identities in relation to others that might create discord, both among members of a challenging group and within self-understandings. This is true for matters of ontology as well as strategy. This ambiguity also provides opportunities for challengers within to partly refashion institutional narratives, a key aspect of the project of being faithful Catholics that the St. Erasmus VOTFers pursued at various times.

The construction of collective identities through stories becomes especially consequential for contention when actors see a problematic fit between the canonical, institutional stories used to organize and explain action and events unfolding around them.[17] Challengers can transpose stories between or within institutions for critique and posing alternatives.[18] In such cases challengers often rework familiar story lines to create paths for their evolving identities and those of their emerging antagonists, as well as to offer evaluative criteria for future action. Storytelling provides the traction to stay on a path of redress when the dilemmas of identity threaten its perceived stability.

One dimension of this traction is the continuing production of collective efficacy.[19] Stories can affirm collective efficacy in the flow of ongoing action. Their sense making provides collective actors with plausible accounts of how, why, and when their actions can make a difference. For challengers within more particularly, the appropriation of institutional narratives allows them to navigate the dilemmic nature of their collective identity as faithful change agents.[20]

Challengers within must simultaneously compose a narrative identity for themselves (as individuals and as a newly constituted group) and rework a narrative account of the larger organization or institution within which they are embedded. Thus the student sit-in protests revised their relationship with adult activists through their narrative.

This narrative work is both ontological and strategic. In terms of the former, actors turn to storytelling to reconstitute their sense of existential traction in an evolving series of events. Through them, they organize and make sense of emotional responses and reconstitute their collective understanding of themselves as principled agents who have the capacity and moral authority to respond. They employ stories to structure paths of redress. We claim that mobilization can be prompted when this ongoing storytelling becomes imperiled, when people face significant risks to the narrative identities that provide them with ontological security.[21]

In our analysis we argue that narrative is an emergent and dialogical process through which challengers within not only produce an ontological narrative but also narrate its change. We call these stories of change "narratives of temporality." The point is that although all stories have beginnings (and middles and ends, for that matter), not all stories are *about* beginnings (or middles or ends). The latter stories—the narratives of temporality—are crucially important in initiating and sustaining collective action. Maintaining livable paths requires narratives of temporality. We see this in terms of what Emirbayer and Mische (1998), in their theorization of agency, describe as "projectivity," the capacity of people to take the iterative aspects of social life and engage in symbolic recomposition.

Most of the narratives that we discuss in the following analysis are canonical. By this we mean that they are widely known and used by group members to provide for ontological security, moral guidance, a sense of collective identity, a location in a flow of time, and a means through which members jointly consider their actions. Narrative theorists have made similar arguments in their discussions of the ways stories are formulated, accumulated, and transformed, and the way people draw on narratives for action. Arthur Frank (2012), for example, observes that people have a narrative habitus of expected and understood plotlines that is maintained in what he calls an "inner library" of narratives. This inner library provides the framework of emplotments for understanding known stories as well as how people can interpret and incorporate new stories. He and the cultural psychologist James Wertsch suggest that this repertoire of narratives serves as a set of "schematic narrative templates" through which remembering and projectivity are organized and made actionable (Wertsch 2002, 62).[22]

In the analyses below, most of the group stories we examine were part of this repertoire of templates, an inner library, on which St. Erasmus VOTFers drew both in their interviews with us and in their public deliberations. While we make reference to a particular telling, each case represents part of a canon that we heard repeated (though not always in identical fashion) elsewhere.

Methods and Microfoundations

To analyze these dynamics of identity work we "go small." Gary Alan Fine characterizes the small group as a "tiny public for the purposes of civic engagement" and notes, "It is on the level of the small groups that things happen" (2012, 1, 20). Groups are the foundation for contention because they provide the bases of solidarity, identity, and trust; a shared past; a means of constructing boundaries; and systems of meaning for action. Activist careers are launched, and sustained, by little actions that provide new ways of responding to dominant power. Storied action unfolds as group members confront the bounded ambiguity of the present and imagine the path of redress forward for their project. This is what Jeffrey Goldfarb (2006) terms the "politics of small things." He argues that the many discussions around kitchen tables in 1980s Poland that were the precursors of the Solidarity movement are exemplary. With similar purpose, Belinda Robnett (1996), in her signal reclamation of women's leadership in the civil rights movement, demonstrates how activists such as Septima Clark engaged with small Southern communities to reimagine and reorganize their freedom project. Of course all groups operate within macro contexts that bound the possibilities for contention, but to gain a complete understanding of the course of contention we need to analyze both top-down and bottom-up analyses of power, as Tilly (1998, 2008) long advocated. To analyze the ontological dimensions of contention that we explore requires scrutiny of small-group dynamics.

We thus see going small not as a narrowing of scope but as a shift in orientation in order to focus on the recursive dynamics of agency and identity. St. Erasmus VOTFers gathered around tables weekly to negotiate the delicate politics of being faithful Catholics. To understand how they managed their identities, how they persevered in the face of hostility, and how they found themselves on a path that they certainly had not imagined requires going small.

The intellectual purchase of focusing on a single affiliate of the Voice of the Faithful is that it enabled us to "burrow" into the group and watch it develop over time (Fine 2010). This research does not purport to explain anything about the national VOTF organization. The larger organization certainly figures into the story of the St. Erasmus affiliate insofar as the members of St. Erasmus acknowledge they are part of the larger organization. At the same time, they experience their own group as distinctive and—at times—opposed to the national organization. Indeed, this local-national boundary within the VOTF is one of many that the St. Erasmus VOTF members find themselves straddling.

We not only went small, we went long. We began our ethnography in June 2007. One of the last gatherings we attended—an informal lunch with about ten people—took place in November 2017. During the first two years of our research, our interactions and observations with the group were intensive and varied. During that time both of us attended every weekly meeting. Each meeting involved a formal program such as an invited speaker, a break out of the working groups, and discussion of a reading or film, and ended with informal refreshments. In addition to the weekly meetings at St. Erasmus, we attended the monthly steering committee meetings (open to all members, but attended by a core of approximately ten), as well as the national conference of the Voice of the Faithful. On a few occasions we attended meetings of other local affiliates, typically when members of St. Erasmus indicated their interest and intention to attend. We also took part in the annual events hosted by St. Erasmus VOTF to support priests of integrity and the annual anniversary commemoration, and we had numerous casual dinners and lunches with individual members.

Although this intense period of observation lasted only two years, we continued to attend three or four meetings every year as well as the summer cookout for priests until 2017. We were also invited to speak to the group about our research almost every year and we used these invitations as opportunities to prompt discussion and reflection from the group. For instance, after we came to understand the significance of Vatican II as a warrant for their activism, we were able to further explore the meaning of this event for the group during one meeting at which we spoke. We were thus able to share and refine our own emergent understanding of their experience. We also examined VOTF newsletters, films, handouts, discussion prompts, and books, including a collection entitled *Voices: Telling Our Stories*, edited and published by the national organization but including many accounts from St. Erasmus members.

The observational and archival data were augmented by semistructured interviews of the core members of this affiliate about their lives as Catholics, their reaction to the sexual abuse scandal, specifically, and to the Catholic Church more generally, and their ongoing efforts to change the Church. The interviews lasted between two and three hours and were conducted early in our research. The purposes of the interviews were twofold. They gave us an opportunity to learn about individuals' autobiographies (as Catholics and activists) and to gather information about the first five years of the affiliate. Less structured "conversations" about many of these issues continued over the years.

Since the purpose of this research was to identify the processes through which activists make sense of their own activism, both individually and collectively, we used a variant of interpretive phenomenological analysis (IPA) (Smith, Flowers, and Larkin 1999) and narrative analysis. Both IPA and narrative analysis are based on the proposition that understanding phenomena requires attending to the ways in which subjects interpret their lived experiences and in doing so come to constitute their lifeworld. Both IPA and narrative analysis implicate a double hermeneutic insofar as in each the researcher is in effect "making sense" of the participants "making sense." Since storytelling is an important means for sense making and sense claiming, each interview was read in its entirety, with attention to the narratives embedded in the accounts. We then wrote a summary of each interview, in effect writing our own second-order narrative: abstracting events mentioned, placing them in some chronological and causal order. We conducted a similar analysis of our field notes, paying particular attention to the process of mutual storytelling within the group. We noted, for instance, the frequency with which collective stories were told and when they were revised or displaced by newer stories as the focal concerns of the group shifted. The narratives, as well as the "work" they accomplished in constructing the identity of St. Erasmus VOTF, serve as the analytical basis of the chapters that follow.

Over the course of our eleven-year engagement with the St. Erasmus VOTF group members often asked us how and why we chose them to study. In fact, our initial interest in the question of how faithful insiders become activists did not involve the sex scandal or Voice of the Faithful. Rather it concerned Catholics who—in cities across the state—were occupying churches slated for closure by the Catholic Church. In the course of identifying a potential research site for that project, we learned about the Voice of the Faithful—a group that in aiming to change the Catholic Church was adopting much more ambitious and undefined goals than preserving a single parish church. While our interest in the analytic question of collective identity remained we thus pivoted from one movement to another.

Identifying a particular affiliate to study was initially somewhat arbitrary but, as with so much in life, proved to be fateful. A quick internet search for a VOTF meeting to attend yielded what appeared to be an incredibly active group with weekly postings announcing lectures, plays, or other events. While other affiliates of the VOTF were waning (or banned) we happened upon one of the most active and, as it turned out, long-lived affiliates. This enabled us to address questions regarding how groups endure and what role identity plays in that process.

The meetings were "open to the public" so we decided to drop in unannounced and establish contact with the group organizer or leader. The first week we showed up in 2007 to learn more about the organization and to talk to them about the possibility of our studying them, St. Erasmus VOTF was sponsoring a one-woman play about the life of St. Catherine of Siena that was held in the church nave, rather than the basement hall where they regularly met. There were more than three hundred people that particular Monday night, a crowd that, as we would discover, was highly unusual.

We also learned that there is no formal organizational structure to the affiliate and we thus were unsure of whom to approach about our interest in studying the group. During the week after the play, we wrote to the man who introduced the one-woman play, Peter Hall. Peter was, in fact, the informal but widely acknowledged and respected leader. He expressed his willingness to ask the members at the next steering committee meeting. Their response was cautiously positive. Having been denounced by some fellow Catholics, they were understandably alert to the downside of exposure and perhaps not entirely sure of our motives. We were subsequently told by members present at the steering committee meeting that Peter's endorsement was critical in securing entrée. We agreed to change the name and not disclose the location of the affiliate. All individuals too have been given pseudonyms.

Because our relationship with the group grew into one of mutual trust and respect, it soon became apparent that exiting the field would be more difficult than entering had been. But this too turned out to be both personally fulfilling and analytically beneficial. Had we limited our observations to only one or two years we would have missed crucial turning points in the construction of their identity. Indeed, our model of collective identity as a product of managing identity "crises" only emerged after witnessing a number of such threats over the years.

We are not sure why Peter did support our research, but we like to think it was because he was aware of the importance of storytelling in sustaining the vitality of a group and we appeared on the scene as a rapt audience to their ongoing story.

Conclusion

The dominant model of contentious action illuminates how groups make fateful decisions but does not fully explain what animates them. We suggest that a shift to the pragmatic and the phenomenological reveals an ongoing ontological project not captured by this approach. We see groups as emergent flows of activity whose coordinated efforts are as much about the process of realizing who they are in the world through their actions as about how these actions will get them to a desired goal. We argue that those desired goals partly are a product of fluid processes by which activists forge a path of redress. Challengers within face a particularly complex set of circumstances as they seek both continuity and change.

This is particularly the case for the ways in which they negotiate the identity work through which they evaluate their project. Overall, we offer an addition to current perspectives on identity work that focuses on the existential dimensions of collective identity, the ways in which challengers work through dilemmas, contradictions, and ambiguity in identity work. For St. Erasmus VOTFers, being faithful Catholics involved feelings and understandings of belonging, worth, morality, and well-being. Their identity process was dilemmic in that members always confronted their standing in their own eyes and those of others as encompassing both sameness and otherness. In the identity process St. Erasmus VOTFers both reacted to those definitions as articulated by others and injected their own meanings into these terms. In the analysis ahead we focus on the evolving existential aspects of identity processes and demonstrate how they were dialogic.[23]

Much of the identity work we witnessed was carried out through narrative. As an increasing number of analysts emphasize, it is not only what the stories tell us, but the work members do through them, that is significant. Stories provide an interpretive lens through which action can be oriented and by which novel events can be made familiar. They offer culturally resonant schema that provide models of social organization and action and a vision of the past, present, and future. We participate in institutions by placing ourselves within their story lines that serve as a template for action. The process of storytelling contains essential ambiguity that elicits participation and the telling of more tales. Narrative is also one of the principal activities through which we construct and maintain our identities.

In this study we explore how the process of storytelling provided members with mobility and traction along an uncertain path of redress. Much of the work on narratives and social movements has focused on stories of origins and how they provide challengers a vehicle to coalesce around a shared sense of purpose and agency and a desired future. From our emergentist perspective we explore how the storytelling of St. Erasmus VOTFers was a dynamic process of identity, a way of navigating shifting relationships (both internal and external), and an ongoing effort to live their moral careers and make the future explicable as circumstances changed. Culture is not consensual or fixed, nor does it stand alone and channel group action. Activist groups push for shared definitions and meanings, but these are "never fully accomplished and always emergent" (Blee 2012, 31). We are thus as much interested in successor as origin stories.

Following from these considerations, the St. Erasmus VOTFers demonstrate the possibilities for other emergentist analyses of collective challenge. At the group level, purpose, solidarity, identity, understandings of the past, present, and future, and many other aspects of activism are "ever being made." The path of these challengers within demonstrates that attention to this unfolding on the micro level enriches our understanding of the dynamics of social change writ large.

Constructing Collective Identity

Under usual conditions, the penitent enters the confessional and kneels behind a curtain or screen so as to conceal his identity. After beginning with the Sign of the Cross, the confessor may share a passage from Sacred Scripture. Then, the penitent uses the familiar formula, "Bless/Forgive me, Father, for I have sinned. It has been __ weeks/months/years since my last Confession." Next, the penitent honestly names the sins of which he is guilty. He may conclude the recital of his sins by asserting, "I am sorry for these and for all the sins of my past life." The confessor gives some valuable counsel to the penitent, encouraging him to put his trust in God and seek true Christian holiness. The confessor also assigns a penance which is to help repair the injustice which the penitent has caused by his sins.[1]

The faithful formed two long lines inside Sacred Heart Church on a Friday afternoon last month, some waiting as long as two and a half hours to step into the confessional where they whispered their sins through the blue curtain to the Rev. Jesus Reynaga—the lone pastor in this humble parish. . . . Father Reynaga's Hispanic parishioners, many of them immigrants without legal status, have much faith and many problems, he said, and they all come to him. . . . "I tell them, 'Please, tell me only your sins. Don't tell me your stories.'"[2]

In many ways, the traditional practice of confession in the Catholic Church epitomized the standing of the laity in relation to the clergy. Highly scripted, mandated weekly, and conducted anonymously, confession, as sociologist of religion Enzo Pace notes, was "one of the mechanisms by which the Church formerly patrolled its moral and theological boundaries" (2007, 39). Yet, to scholars interested in the role of narrative in constituting identity and motivating action, what is most striking about this model of a good confession is the complete absence of the narrative form. Sins are to be enumerated, along with their frequency, not in order of occurrence—first this, then that—but recited in descending order of gravity. There is no opportunity to account for context, motive, extenuating or aggravating circumstances, causes, or effects. The passage of time is noted only in relation to the last confession. In the context of the interaction, the penitent—whose identity is traditionally concealed—becomes the sum of his sins, multiplied by their frequency (plus all of the sins of his past life). With absolution, the penitent, now sinless, has no history, no past. In short, devoid of character, plot, or temporality, a "good" confession renders the Catholic penitent storyless before the priest.

It is not just the traditional practice of confession that deprived lay Catholics of the opportunity to tell a story, or have that story heard. Many of the traditional practices of the Church rendered the laity silent. The pre-Vatican II Mass was delivered in Latin and was thus incomprehensible to the parishioners. James Carroll described the Latin Mass as "the ingenious Roman Tongue that had, across the centuries, rendered the people mute" (2009, 128). One member of St. Erasmus VOTF echoed this sentiment. "In those days Mass was in Latin, so 'what's going on anyways?'" Even with the adoption of the vernacular Mass and the reorientation of the altar so that the priest faced the worshippers, there was little opportunity for lay Catholics to engage in real conversation. "Well, how much dialogue is there in Sunday Mass? I mean, it was radical in Vatican II to get people participating by *singing*."

These traditions laid the foundations for VOTF's assertion of a voice into a radical challenge. Phil Harper spoke often of the silencing of Catholics. Phil was a former priest who entered the seminary in his teens. He spent time in Africa and later working at a hospital in a deep Southern city. He was impressed with the expressive and relational nature of religious worship in Africa. "It was holiness and energy and spiritual gathering and pulling people together. The ritual was a way of helping people celebrate life together. The important thing is that they're together, not that they are Christian or Catholic." By contrast, "The Catholic Church for so long has had this attitude that you can't talk. There are huge things we're not supposed to talk about. In a culture where talk is forbidden, talk can become very dangerous." While working in a hospital Phil also learned the power of dialogue and connection. He told us that when he started working there he really wanted to "bring the Eucharist" to the sick and dying, a distinctive prerogative of the clergy. "But the older priests in New Orleans said 'Forget the Eucharist.' They said 'Talk to them.' It's talking about relationship and being with each other as opposed to dogma from top down. It's about talking. Dialogue, collegiality." Phil eventually decided to leave the priesthood. Although this was a difficult decision, he did not experience it as a failure, more a change in direction. He realized that "I can't do anything to break my relationship with God. That's taken care of. So all I've got to do is figure out how I am going to live my life. It became quite optional for me which way I could go. I could either go [leave the priesthood] or I could stay."

Like other members of St. Erasmus VOTF, Phil's reaction to the abuse revelation was not immediate. He refers to himself as "cynically naive"—a contradiction that aptly describes many of the activists—and characterizes his involvement in the group as gradual. He attributes this to the fact that as a result of his Catholic upbringing he has difficulty expressing anger.

So in relation to the crisis, I think in that first instance it was kind of like "Of course, this was going on." But then I think what really struck me more than anything else was [through talking in early listening sessions] the depth of the destruction of the abuse and the effects.

The word *faithful,* when attached to Catholic laity, has historically expressed an expectation of obedience and deference to Church clergy, hierarchy, and dogma—an expectation that still existed in some form in 2002. This was exemplified at the turn of the twentieth century, when Pope Leo XIII denounced what he called "Americanism" as the "synthesis of all heresies"—indicting in particular the First Amendment to the United States Constitution. Although Vatican II reversed Pope Leo's condemnation of freedom of speech and thought and affirmed the primacy of individual conscience, a conservative reaction to this revision soon emerged. According to James Carroll, "Within Roman Catholicism, the conservative reaction against the reforms of Vatican II can be understood as a 're-Catholicization,' an attempt to restore the Church of the antimodernist nineteenth century, if not of the Middle Ages" (2009, 253).

Many of the members of St. Erasmus VOTF grew up well before Vatican II. They acquired their Catholic identity within the enclaves of the local parish, where the Church and, more immediately, the parish priests and nuns (for whom deference was a habit) shaped almost every aspect of their daily life. Their Catholic identity was, and remains, a cherished and meaningful part of their sense of the world and self, of right and wrong, of justice and injustice. It is against this historical and biographical background that St. Erasmus VOTFers faced the prospect of speaking out and taking action in the wake of the abuse scandal and cover-up.

In the months after the scandal broke almost everyone in the group eventually knew that they needed to do something, but at the onset hardly any of them knew what that something was or should be. Initially, they thought that the Church hierarchy would welcome their assistance in reforming the Church, in effect addressing the crisis. When they met with resistance and censure from both the clergy and from fellow Catholics, they quickly redefined their project and, in the process, reformulated their identity. The rapid adoption of the three goals by the national group—supporting survivors of sexual abuse, supporting priests of integrity, and bringing about structural change within the Church—named but did not define what the work of the group would be. They still had to figure out what might constitute structural change. Who are priests of integrity? What kind of support do the priests need and what kind can we offer? And, most important, what would an adequate response to the survivors entail?

Looking back over the past decade, many VOTFers note that the group's project has evolved into one dedicated to dialogue, education, and self-constitution. The early emotions that fueled their reaction to the scandal have seasoned to something more akin to conviction. Their initial discomfort in challenging the hierarchy and attracting the censure of some fellow Catholics has transformed into collective pride, efficacy, and honor; some have even characterized it as the "cross" they bear for the Church. Some have expressed frustration or resignation regarding what they see as the turning away from their initial commitment to "change the Church." Others recognize that their initial project of changing the Church has not been replaced by—as much as realized in—their efforts at dialogue and education. Rather than simply changing the Church to accommodate a more active and empowered laity, they have become a more active and empowered laity.

We rely on stories and invest them with great significance in our account of St. Erasmus VOTF. In part, this is because the system of abuse itself was a result of the failure of storytelling and narrative. The story the victims had to tell was so painful and unimaginable to others that many never shared it with anyone it until decades later.[3] In some cases, parents and teachers disbelieved those who did tell their story of abuse at the time it occurred. For its part, the Church hierarchy either refused to hear the victims who came forward or imposed gag orders on those to whom they finally granted a hearing.

We also rely on narrative in this account because stories are a critical vehicle through which culture and identity are activated. This is not to say that storytelling is inherently liberatory (Ewick and Silbey 1995). Narratives can become a means through which control is exercised, inequality justified, fear perpetuated, and conformity secured. Still, the power of narrative to convey and invent meaning suggests that as a *form* it contains the potential for remaking the world, for staking a claim about what matters and why. If narrative, then, has any liberatory quality, it lies in this: the ability to tell a story, and thus to have a voice. Even if (inevitably) the narrative is fashioned out of what is at hand—that is, the stories that others have told before—this ability makes a possible world legible and meaningful.

It is not only the storyteller who reimagines worlds. Every story needs an audience. It is the audience who (ironically) "authorizes" the story and, in doing so, enables its world-making capacity. It is not simply the ability to tell a story that liberates and empowers, it is the possibility of it being heard. For this reason, the story we are about to tell about Voice of the Faithful is as much about the role of listening as it is telling. Bearing witness, hearing stories, and retelling stories are central and, in the context of the Church, radical parts of what they did. Hearing the victims' agony and hearing the priests' stories of loneliness and ostracism were painful and difficult parts of their work. After a lifetime of not being allowed to speak, they offered to listen to others speak.

I can remember not particularly liking the term "voice of the faithful" when it was first chosen. I am not sure why. But now I really, really believe that it was providential. In a sense of, if I were to describe any relationship, it is in finding my voice. It's interesting how we give each other the ability to find our voices. Nobody can find it without other people. What's missing still is the fact that we are not able to do it with the whole faithful. (Phil)

From one angle, the work of St. Erasmus VOTF has been to participate in being storied Catholics: to hear and to tell stories that would be heard. To some extent, this has entailed writing and enacting new stories of their past, present, and future. It has necessitated rescripting traditional accounts of the Church. It has also involved bearing witness to the stories others have to tell: survivors and priests. Much of the storytelling of VOTFers has been narrating themselves to themselves, creating characters and plots in which they endowed themselves with the capacity, efficacy, and authority to change the Church. They discovered that their work of remaking the Church was predicated on their work of remaking themselves. Although they set out to change the Church, in their efforts they also engaged in changing themselves.

Much of the group's initial identity work was in response to the discontinuity they experienced between their pasts as passive and faithful Catholics and their nascent activism. By narrating this transformation, they constructed an identity that was both totally new and at the same time firmly rooted in their past. Indeed, generally part of becoming an activist—or anything new and different—entails revising a life history but not jettisoning it.

With time, other aspects of their collective identity became problematic. As a group attempting to change the Church, they were depicted as outsiders, dissidents, and troublemakers by many parishioners, other conservative Catholic groups, and some clergy. In contrast to many newly formed change groups that strove to construct group boundaries in order to highlight their distinctiveness, St. Erasmus VOTF reacted to these critics by asserting their similarity with other Catholics while remaining steadfast in their commitment to changing the Church. After a lifetime of identifying as faithful Catholics, their challenge early on was to secure recognition and affirmation of their activism and faith from precisely those who would criticize or denounce their mission.

Their eventual success in achieving recognition as faithful Catholics who were seeking change did not settle their identity as much as it shifted the focus internally. Having secured affirmation from others within the Church, differences among VOTF members—particularly regarding the priority of the three goals—emerged as the most troublesome identity issue. In order to manage the tensions of internal difference and discord, the members of St. Erasmus needed to formulate stories and identity practices that would integrate, without eliminating, the differences among the members. The remarkable persistence of this group is in large part, we argue, a measure of their ability to address and manage the ongoing tensions inherent in the project of their identity.

Many of the stories told by the St. Erasmus VOTFers explicitly or implicitly involved encounters with authority. Most obviously, this was the case in addressing the role of the transgressive priests and the hierarchy involved in the cover-up. However, narrating their relationships with survivors, Church officials, and even one another all necessitated some accounting of the role of authority. In these stories, what Foucault called "pastoral power" casts a strong shadow over the ways in which the abuse crisis and responses to it should be understood.[4] Foucault defined pastoral power as "a power of care. It looks after the flock, it looks after the individuals of the flock, it sees to it that the sheep does not suffer, it goes in search of those that have strayed off course, and it treats those that are injured" (2007, 127). He claimed that pastoral power is distinguished by three features. First, it is exercised over people, rather than over territory. Second, it is committed to salvation (*salut*, or safety and protection from harm in a more secular translation) of the people. Finally, it is individualizing insofar as it attends to the needs of the entire flock, while making sure that not a single sheep escapes (Welch 2010). "It is therefore a power with a purpose for those on whom it is exercised, not a purpose for some kind of superior unit like the city, territory, state, or sovereign" (Foucault 2007, 129).

The figurative use of the shepherd tending the flock has been long used as a model of Catholic community and remains relevant in the modern Church (Loveland and Ksander 2014). In the *Lumen gentium* of Vatican II, for example, the Church is characterized as a sheepfold or cultivated field rather than as an institution or formal organization (Curran 2011, 41). Although Foucault did not see pastoral power as relevant only in religious institutions (indeed, as it entered politics, it led to the formation of the modern state), its connection to VOTF and the Catholic Church is manifest. In many ways, to members of VOTF the scandal represents the failure of the Church to exercise pastoral power (by failing to protect the victims of abuse and covering up the crimes of clergy) and their own activism represents an assumption of that responsibility. As Foucault noted in a different context, "Critics of the Church that fails its obligations reject its hierarchical structure, look for more or less spontaneous forms of community in which the flock could find the shepherd it needed" (1994, 313). While most of members of St. Erasmus VOTF did not entirely reject the Church hierarchy and its dogmatic claims to authority, part of their emergence, as we discuss in subsequent chapters, involved pragmatically engaging new modes of shepherding, both with survivors and among themselves. Ultimately, as we discuss in later chapters, this led them to see how the flock can shepherd itself.

This emergent and reflexive narration of authority relations suffused their dialogic accounts of all three axes of identity: temporality, external relations, and internal relations. In the following three chapters we take each in turn.

TWO

Narrating Rupture and Continuity

Thomas McNally is a passionate advocate for survivors of clergy sexual abuse and for the protection of children. His commitment to those issues sometimes leaves him frustrated with VOTF's focus on structural change and the support of priests of integrity—what he sees as important but less central goals. Tall and lean with a weathered face, he is a soft-spoken iconoclast. If VOTF is, as some have claimed, the conscience of the Church, Thomas is a conscience of VOTF. As is often the case with those who assume the role of a conscience, his unrelenting support for victims can cause some discomfort and resentment on the part of others who are put off by his "fury."

Thomas traces his involvement with the VOTF and other activist groups to his relationship to his grandchildren.

I have four grandchildren. You know how you make up these stories that explain [your life]?)—Well, my mother was a person who had a natural relationship with children, almost a relationship of equality. . . . As I got older I just watched and watched her ability to very quickly form relations with children. I presume it flows in through the pores or something, [because] when my first grandson was born I had *the same relationship*. I can also relate to children. In a way that just shocked me. I mean I laugh. I used to hear stories about grandparents and grandchildren and I thought it was a big joke. And then my grandson came along and I said "no, I'm the joke."

At this point, Thomas pauses and thinks about how old his grandson was when the *Globe* story broke: "about five, just like some of the victims were when they were abused." He then wonders, "What kind of adult are you after experiencing that? When I talk to survivors, I can see the child. The child is there."

Since joining Voice of the Faithful, Thomas has demonstrated on behalf of survivors every Sunday morning in front of a main archdiocesan cathedral. He describes the first time he went to protest and how it changed him:

So I go to the cathedral. I walk up and there's this howling mob of people standing outside with bull horns yelling things that . . . well, you can't say that. And you know, within a month *I'm* one of the howlers and yellers. You absorb the sense of outrage at what [the Church hierarchy] are doing. And what they continue to do, and the fact that they are never willing to admit that what they're doing is grossly immoral. It's criminal. It's awful.

Having "absorbed that sense of outrage," Thomas is dogged and strategic in his efforts to keep attention on the plight of survivors. In addition to his weekly demonstrations at the cathedral, he also organizes ad hoc demonstrations when opportunities present themselves, such as installations of new bishops, papal visits—or even at a national VOTF conference where he once protested what he saw as insufficient attention to victims of abuse by organizing a demonstration on the sidewalk outside the conference hall. Thomas is also a major actor in another organization devoted to survivor issues. If he is provocative, he is self-consciously so, at one point describing himself as "a fly at the beach that keeps buzzing around."

I made a determination that any time that I can get anywhere near one of those things [bishop installations], they're not going to have a procession without seeing the faces of those children [photos of victims on placards]. There is not going to be any event where they're going to go parading around in robes where we're not going to be there.

Thomas also works hard to incite others to demonstrate on behalf of victims, but he is often disappointed in their response to his call to action. Recalling a meeting where he had appealed to people to show up at a demonstration the next day, he spoke of the group's responsibility "to be present the way Jesus was present in his day." He then sighed and said, "I believe out of a group of 250 people, ten people came the next day."

Despite his unwavering commitment to hold the Church hierarchy accountable at every opportunity, Thomas is also a deeply committed Catholic whose religious faith has withstood the scandal—in some ways growing stronger. In this regard, Thomas shares the dilemma most of the group faces: how to remain faithful Catholics as they confront what they see as a serious betrayal by the hierarchy and a compromising of the Church. He explains his activism as an obligation of his faith rather than a betrayal of it.

My practice has certainly changed [since the sex abuse scandal]. A lot. I believe that faith is a gift and you get the gift. And not only that but then you are given the grace to accept the gift. . . . The message that I think that you're supposed to get is that Jesus died for your sins. You're saved. And all the rest of the stuff about having to go to church or having to do this or not do that. Wrong message. You are saved. However, you need to respond. You are made an offer. Accepting of the offer is that you live that life. It's not what you say, it's what you do.

Knowing that you are obligated to respond and knowing how to respond are not the same thing, however. At one meeting Thomas, an experienced sailor, recognizes the ontological and strategic difficulties of this situation by likening the efforts of the group to "fixing a ship at sea."

I don't know if there's anybody else in this room who has ever fixed a ship at sea, but I have done so—it is intense and it is gut-wrenching and, I've got to tell you, it is riveting. I would not advise it. There were times that we had to open the ship more to let more water in, in order to be able to get at the thing that we needed to get at to stop the problem.

Thomas's use of this analogy is stark and telling. It depicts an ongoing process, work that is ontologically "intense" and "gut-wrenching." His account vividly conveys the urgency and the danger entailed in "having to let more water in" and thus risking destroying the very thing he is trying to save. It highlights members' predicament concerning how much to change the institution without destroying that which is essential and valued about it and, as members, themselves. The image also conveys the fusion of one's own fate and identity with that of the Church. Immediately following the revelations of sexual abuse, the members of St. Erasmus grappled with questions such as "What kind of Church is this?" and "What kind of Catholic am I?" In other words, both their ongoing faith and their nascent activism were predicated on "reasonably accounting" for what appeared to be an abrupt and radical transformation in their understanding of the Church and their membership.

The Temporal Dimension of Identity

"What we call the beginning is often the end
And to make an end is to make a beginning."
T. S. ELIOT, "LITTLE GIDDING"

Bellah et. al. note that "Communities . . . have a history—in an important sense are constituted by their past—and for this reason we can speak of a real community as a 'community of memory,' one that does not forget its past" (1985, 153). Yet the past is not a singular repository of experiences or memories; each group has multiple, overlaid pasts reflecting different horizons that appear fixed, in part, on the purposes for which they are retrieved, applied, or reworked. In some cases, pasts are recollected in order to establish continuity, by discovering roots of present action in some prior self or some earlier experiences. Continuity is not always what is sought, however. In some cases, groups excavate a past in part to mark a beginning. The break imparts meaning to the present and future momentum.[1]

In dealing with questions about their ongoing faith and their emerging activism, members of St. Erasmus told two types of stories about time and change, stories that stand in tension with each other. First, they told origin stories about the cataclysmic events that led to the formation of the group. For challengers within, the "beginning" that needs to be explained often represents an event or experience that cannot be subsumed within existing narrative scripts. Such events are a rupture; the origin story is a repair or revitalization. By identifying some situation or event that compels action—in this case the hierarchy's involvement in the sexual abuse of children—these stories lighten the burden of accounting for discontinuity by shifting agency to something external.[2] It is as if these stories say, in effect, *I haven't changed, something out there has.*

Whereas origin stories narrate rupture or a break with the past, successor stories narrate continuity.[3] These stories claim that the roots of VOTF members' activism—of who they are and what they are doing in the present and might do in the future—were always present. Challengers within in particular need to establish such continuity to claim legitimacy and agency.

In the case of VOTF, successor stories took two forms: individual and institutional. The individual stories were accounts of prior experiences and identities in which members stood up to unjust authority. At an institutional level, the successor stories involved the retrieval and retelling of Church history that prefigured their vision of its reformation. In other words, challengers from within organizations and institutions to which they have been and wish to remain loyal must simultaneously compose a narrative identity for themselves and rework a narrative account of the larger organization or institution within which they are embedded.[4] For VOTF, this took the form of constituting themselves as change seekers (after a lifetime of relative passivity and acquiescence to Church authority) and telling a story of the Catholic Church as an institution that, despite present circumstances and scandals, is compatible with and open to their goal of change.

Both origin stories and successor stories represent a kind of template and warrant for their change effort.[5] Furthermore, it is the tension between the two types of stories that provides the narrative arc that constitutes the temporal dimension of identity.[6] As we noted earlier, Giddens (1984) suggests identity is the process of maintaining a story of self. Maintaining it requires, as is true of all narratives, *both* continuity and change.[7] On one hand, identity is based on the sense that who we are—as individuals or as a group—is meaningfully related to our pasts and to who we will be in the future. At the same time, however, a well-formed narrative also requires change, or plot. Keeping the narrative going, therefore, is predicated on narrating continuity in the face of change or rupture. Identity could not exist solely in a situation of perpetual change, but neither could it exist only in a situation of uninterrupted sameness,[8] for in neither case would there be a story.

How It All Began

"Men can do nothing without the make-believe of a beginning."
GEORGE ELIOT

Origin stories are collective narratives in the double sense that they are about the beginning of the group or movement, but also in the sense that in their telling they come to constitute the group. According to Alfred Schutz, "Communicating with one another presupposed, therefore, the simultaneous partaking of the partners in various dimensions of outer and inner time—in short in growing older together" (1973, 217). We argue that collective identity is forged out of the awareness of this process of "growing older together."[9] This process is often represented in what we called narratives of temporality—or stories of change—and experienced again and again in their retelling.[10] In the personal and collective origin stories we frequently encountered a "before and after," a narrative of temporality that highlighted a fundamental turning point. As one member observed at a meeting, "I was essentially a passive Catholic before then. . . . I mean, you just never questioned anything. You just did the 'pray, pay, and obey' thing." The scandal triggered a process through which identity work became dialogic and the need for recognition of their status within the Church explicit.

Origin stories are distinguished from other forms of everyday storytelling by virtue of the regularity and frequency with which they are told and the similarity in how they are told, as well as their "before and after" division. The constitutive power of origin stories lies in the fact that they transcend historical time, offering a recursive or cyclical understanding of experience. In this sense, origin narratives are less about commemoration—the recollection of a historical event—than they are about reiteration, a return, a circling back along with continued movement. Thus, in addition to imposing coherence on challengers' initial activities and offering a sense of a compelling force behind contention, origin stories allow "the narrators of past events to 'keep doing it until they get it right,' to wrestle with an account of what occurred and what was said until fundamental truths shine through the story" (Engel 1993, 792). The need to keep doing it until they get it right is typically prompted by something going very wrong: an event or experience that is incomprehensible and inconceivable and that incites what Karl Weick has called a sudden loss of meaning in which "present events outstrip past experience" (1993, 636). In the face of such unintelligibility, we ask, "What is the story here?"[11] The answers to that question are the contingent product of sense making, a process in which actors interpret situations, identity, and action. "If the first question of sense-making is 'what's going on here?,' the second equally important question is 'what do I do next?'" (Weick, Sutcliffe, and Obstfeld 2005, 410).

In the case of St. Erasmus VOTF, the loss of meaning began with the initial revelations in the *Boston Globe*. Despite the shocking headlines, for many Boston Catholics the "story" was not immediately apparent. The equivocality of the situation accounted for a range of interpretations and thus reactions and emotions: confusion, disbelief, anger, disgust, and even skepticism. As is often the case in situations of crisis and shock, early efforts at sense making involved telling familiar stories that enabled former lines of action and preserved existing identities and relationships.

Victoria Swingewood was born and raised in a devout Catholic family in England. Her family kneeled together to pray every night before bed and said grace before every meal. She attended Catholic school and was thus marginalized somewhat from her predominantly Protestant neighbors and friends. She married a non-Catholic but with little opposition from her family. They lived in Africa and Asia for her husband's work before settling with their three children in a suburb of Boston where they have lived since that time. At various points Victoria told us that while her faith never faltered she questioned some of the teachings of the Church. As a young woman she received permission from the local priest to attend an ecumenical religious discussion group. She told us that because there were non-Catholics in the discussion group "I felt that I should give the party line and that's when I started thinking that some of these party lines were a bit weird. I had never questioned them before." After settling in the US with her family she taught religious education, and this experience also provoked some questioning. "I found myself really questioning my beliefs because of what you're suddenly teaching five and six year olds."

Still Victoria remained a practicing Catholic and joined the more conservative of the parishes in town. Her response to the revelations of systematic sexual abuse by priests was, like Phil's, gradual. She told us that she thought at first that the reports were just another instance of what she perceived as longstanding anti-Catholic bias on the part of the *Boston Globe*. Years after the story broke, she told us:

You're allowed to laugh at this. It was January 2002. We had been fortunate enough that we'd been on some lovely warm weeks' vacation in the Caribbean or something and we came back to [the news]. And I thought, *Here's the* Boston Globe *again.* You know? *Saying these awful things about the Church.* It must have taken me a week to stop getting mad at the *Globe.*

Paradoxically, Victoria's initial reaction was primed by an earlier case of priest sexual abuse. In 1992, it came to light that Reverend James Porter had molested over a hundred children in southeastern Massachusetts. Porter's crimes were depicted as an isolated and aberrant case. In fact, Victoria had been living next door to Porter's "aunt or great aunt. He used to come a visit her a lot. When it got in the papers I, and another neighbor, had a little conspiracy. We would sort of hide the *Globe.* It might seem wrong, but she was ninety or something. I said, 'here, borrow my *Christian Science Monitor.*' Eventually, she told me he [Porter] had moved to California. And I said, 'Oh, for his health?' and she said 'Oh, yes, Maybe.'"

Victoria's reaction to the Porter case, and initially to the 2002 revelations, were predicated on the fact that no evidence of widespread Church cover-up emerged. For years the Church hierarchy was able to success-fully deflect blame onto the media's—particularly the *Boston Globe's*—bias against the Church. At the time and with great righteousness, Car-dinal Law condemned the paper's coverage: "By all means," he said, "we call down God's power on the media, particularly the *Boston Globe*." In 2002, then Cardinal Joseph Ratzinger observed, "I am personally con-vinced that the constant presence in the press of the sins of Catholic priests, especially in the United States, is a planned campaign" (Carroll 2009, 286). In talking about her initial reactions, Victoria reflected, "We were talking about this [the Porter case] last night at the VOTF meeting. We were saying 'Weren't we stupid to think that it was isolated?'"

Margaret Scanlon is also an embodiment of that naive cynicism that Phil mentioned. Margaret is a wiry, athletic, quiet woman who in her eighties plays tennis or golf every day. A former teacher, she still teaches religious education in St. Erasmus's parish and would often leave class on Monday night to come directly to the VOTF meeting in the base-ment. Her reaction to the scandal was more immediate and intense than many. Describing the early meetings she attended at St. Erasmus she said

There was total dismay that we had allowed this to happen. As reasonable adults that allowed this to happen. And that the hierarchy had conspired to hide it. I guess I was also annoyed that people were annoyed at the *Boston Globe*. I know it has an anti-Catholic bent. But so what? This had nothing to do with anti-Catholic. This was just plain wrong.

Moral Shock and Sense Making

As the details of the abuse and cover-up were filled in, most people de-scribed being in a state of what James Jasper (1997) has called "moral shock." Joe, a lifelong Catholic in his seventies and a regular member of St. Erasmus VOTF, expressed the sentiments of many when he described his first reaction to the charge that there was widespread sexual abuse and institutional cover-up: "I felt a little bit that we were being pushed off a cliff." Joe's sense of being "pushed off a cliff" captures a distinctive register of emotion and temporality characteristic of being in crisis. The ground that supports identity and marks a path forward was gone.[12] In a phenom-enological sense, such a crisis represents a suspension—temporarily "not being." At such moments of crisis, the present is foregrounded—falling off a metaphoric cliff, one does not recollect the past or plan the future. Although there is urgency and an overwhelming sense that something must be done, one does not search in any pragmatic way for a solution or adopt a goal. One reaches, gropes, grasps. Experiencing such temporal displacement is characteristic of what Anthony Giddens has called "ontological insecurity." A person experiencing it "lacks a consistent feeling of biographical continuity. . . . Time may be comprehended as a series of discrete moments, each of which severs prior experiences from subsequent ones in such a way that no 'narrative' can be sustained" (1991, 53).

It was in this context of ontological crisis that word soon spread among Catholics in the Boston area about the meetings being held at St. John's in Wellesley, Massachusetts. These started as informal listening sessions at the suggestion of the parish pastor, though they grew into more formal affairs. Many came to those early meetings to express what one of the leaders of the St. Erasmus group termed "white-hot anger" and deep sorrow about the clergy sexual abuse scandal. When we asked Loretta about her initial reactions she responded, "Just, you know, horror, disgust that this kind of thing could go on." Shirley became visibly agitated in remembering those early events: "And this type of thing was just, it was an outrage. It was like a virus infecting your home. . . . I was so angry when all of this happened. It's just something that you can't tolerate in an institution you want to claim." Apprehending the seriousness and the scope of the betrayal, they came to understand that *something* had to be done. After a lifetime of obedience and deference to the Church, they realized that they would have to do it.

According to Jasper and Poulsen (1995), moral shock "inclines" people to action, particularly in the absence of social networks through which activists can be recruited. This depiction seems to describe the formation of the St. Erasmus chapter of VOTF. They were, by their own accounts, in a state of shock and confusion; most lacked experiences of social activism. The problem with the concept of moral shock as an impetus to social activism is that it replicates, rather than illuminates, a common feature of movement origin stories. Activists often write themselves out of the origin script by endowing the situation with the power to compel action. As is the case with many origin stories, members of St. Erasmus VOTF recalled being "pushed" both figuratively and literally. According to Phil, "The tragedy pushed us." Sister Bridget recounted the way in which she was similarly "pushed" into the meeting by the strong wind that came out of nowhere on a calm June evening in the parking lot of St. John's parish.

These origin stories, like Jasper's concept of moral shock, identify some external event as the trigger to action and thus mask the reconfiguration of self (or group) and situation that is necessary if a sustained challenge is to emerge. Jack Katz has written of the ways in which nonroutine action—from falling in love to committing a violent crime—is predicated on what he calls "the pacification of subjectivity," or an abdication of our will to the dynamics of the situation. "What phenomenology has uniquely appreciated is not simply that a person's lived world is his artifact but that by experiencing himself as an object controlled by transcendent forces, an individual can genuinely experience a new or different world. By pacifying his subjectivity, a person can conjure up a magic so powerful that it can change his ontology" (1988, 8).

The organizing, planning, and preliminary staging required in mobilizing are edited out so that the line between "subject and object, being in control and out of control, between directing and being directed by the dynamics of the situation" are redrawn (Katz 1988, 8). Persons become objects that are "seized," "caught up," "swept away," or "pushed" (Polletta 2006; Armstrong and Crage 2006). In other words, in the beginning, becoming agentic—in this case, joining a movement and calling for fundamental change within the Church—requires the narrative denial of agency. The transformative magic of origin stories is contingent, in other words, upon its remaining unperceived and thus un-narrated. Polletta referred to this narrative absence as "the ellipsis," or that which "contains without explaining the unexplainable point at which protest began," concluding that out of these stories new collective actors and collective stakes emerge (2006, 46). The language of sense making, rather than that of moral shock, opens up that ellipsis insofar as it "captures the realities of agency, flow, equivocality, transience, reaccomplishment, unfolding, and emergence" (Weick, Sutcliffe, and Obstfeld. 2005, 410). It acknowledges the suspension of identity that precludes action while recognizing the constitutive magic of narrating one's loss.

The effort to write plausible stories of what was happening continued even after the initial meetings in Wellesley. In part this was due to the fact that the strength of many of our subjects' outrage and disgust at the revelations in the *Globe* were not matched by their resolve to become activists. All but one of those we interviewed offered us autobiographies of long and continuous years as regular churchgoers and active parishioners, emphasizing that their Catholicism was central to their life stories. The individual profiles of the vast majority of the members indicate little to no prior activist experience. In fact, several members explicitly emphasized that they faced internal struggles taking their first participatory steps. Sarah Fauteux grew up in an upper middle class Catholic family, attended Catholic private schools, and eventually graduated from Boston College. When we asked her to explain her involvement she responded, "I ask myself this question because I'm not a joiner. I'm definitely not. My favorite place to be, especially at night, is home, reading my book. . . . I'm serious." Yet despite this reluctance, she accompanied Sister Bridget to the Wellesley session on that warm June evening. Put off by the emotion and anger she witnessed, she remained perplexed as to why she continued to attend meetings of VOTF.

I think we all thought that we would be able to do something. I am not crazy about free range meetings. So in spite of the fact that there were times when I was going nuts, I kept going. And you ask me why, and I asked myself. It is possible that I began to realize how far away from Vatican II that things had gone. So it probably expanded from the abuse crisis for me to Church in general.

Grace, in telling her story, was similarly forthright about her reluctance to get involved, noting that she did not attend the early sessions for several months. "God. I fought it too. And I didn't want to do it at all. As I said, I don't do change very well and I'm not a rabble-rouser at all." In speaking about her early reactions to the St. Erasmus listening sessions she recollected: "I remember going home from these listening sessions and saying I wish I hadn't known what other people were thinking about. . . . I was happier when it was quiet, you know. And that you could kneel down next to somebody in church and you didn't know what they were thinking."

If few of the members of St. Erasmus VOTF could look back and trace the roots of their activism, even fewer could project a future path in this early period. But according to Victoria, as her anger grew, so did her general commitment to change: "Something should be done to change the Church. Something should be done about all those priests who are not reporting. Something should be done to . . . get rid of all those people who covered up. . . . I don't think I had a plan. I did not have a plan, you know." Barb similarly recollected that her initial motivation was simply that "something had to be done." She explained, "We were forming into a group with some idea of what we were trying to do. But I don't think we really knew what we were trying to do. But the thing that happened was the group dynamic. This was the mission at that point."

Despite the ambiguity of their goals, many initially anticipated that VOTF would achieve its purpose in a couple of years. Shirley recalled her sense that the organization would be of short duration: "[F]rom the beginning I've been hoping that it was going to have a term limit. Because my idea was, once the organization started impacting the hierarchy and other members of the Church, that the cause would be so welcomed by the whole Catholic community, you wouldn't need an organization." During one group discussion in the spring of 2009, a key member, Loretta, reflected that she had assumed a five-year time frame to remedy the exposed problems. When one of us asked if they had been naive, the members at the table collectively moaned and replied that *naive* was not strong enough a term.

Indeed, it may have been because of the ambiguity of specific goals that they were able to maintain optimism early on.[13] As opposed to those they saw leaving the Church as a result of the scandal, the St. Erasmus VOTF members conceived of themselves as loyal Catholics whose efforts would be welcomed by the Church—or at least by a Church purged of the guilty priests and bishops. Secure in their loyalty and confident that their efforts would be recognized as an expression of their faith, they assumed the Church would be responsive and even grateful for their efforts. One member thought that the message VOTF was conveying to the Church hierarchy was, "We're your new best friends. We have something to bring to the table." Seeing themselves as loyalists, they did not immediately experience their activism as a dilemma. A measure of their optimism was the fact that few anticipated they would be attending the meetings on a weekly basis for over nine years. The idea that their efforts at changing the Church would be both effective and welcomed by the hierarchy and other mainstream Catholics shortened the temporal horizon of their project and, thus, enabled their participation despite their reluctance and inertia.

Throughout the process of narrating what was happening and what they should do about it, the members of St. Erasmus VOTF were themselves being transformed. The early meetings were large, emotional, and inevitably veered into many issues only tangentially related to the clergy abuse scandal, including the ordination of women, mandatory celibacy, and the role of laity in the Church. As Grace recounted, the very act of speaking and listening irreversibly transformed them. The meetings unleashed what William Gamson (1992) terms "hot cognitions": cognitive evaluations laden with emotions.

I think what happened through the listening sessions that were held is that a lot of people have been thinking about these issues—women priests and celibacy and stuff. And all of a sudden it became okay to talk about them. . . . I keep telling people it's like squeezing the toothpaste tube. You cannot get the toothpaste back in after you've opened it up and squeezed.

In light of the culture of deference and silence within the Church it is not surprising that the emotional tenor of the early meetings was unsettling to many of the VOTF members. As Victoria told us, "Basically, people came and they vented. And people ranted and cried . . . just terribly, terribly raw feelings."[14] Margaret Scanlon recalled that at one meeting where the group was calling for the resignation of Cardinal Law someone stood up and cautioned them that they "were not at a football rally" and urged them to consider that the issues before the group deserved cooler or more deliberate consideration.[15] The contradiction the group faced was how to retain the energy unleashed by the scandal without having the rage and sorrow undermine the work of the group.[16] Emotions such as the ones discussed above are not only combustible, they can also be fragile. Their fragility meant that whatever role emotion played in their resolve to take action could diminish without feeling rules that bounded and channeled structures of affect.

Over the course of our fieldwork we heard various speakers (as well as members) refer to the origin story, including some representatives from the national office of VOTF in Boston. They have highlighted the complexity of maintaining the group's call to purpose while tempering the heat originally experienced. For example, the executive director of the national VOTF noted, "It is difficult to convert a movement—which sprang up out of outrage—into an organization," while a past president observed, "Anger got us going but it cannot sustain us. It will not attract new members. We must move from anger to love."

To some extent the origin story became a means of resolving this dilemma between the combustibility and uncertainty of emotion. On one hand, by continually narrating the beginning of the group, these stories circle back to the initial revelations and keep alive the overwhelming sense of betrayal that "pushed" them to come together. On the other hand, in the repeated telling of the scandal and its effect on them, the story lost its "heat." In many ways, the stories of betrayal, disbelief, and feeling compelled to do something were the opposite of shocking. They became familiar and reassuring accounts of how the group came to be, creating a different emotional foundation for solidarity. Much like the proverbial "family story," the origin stories came to define the group by "collaps[ing] the inquiry of 'where did we come from?' with 'who are we?'" (Silbey 2010, 207). The dual work of the origin story—to keep the memory of shock alive while using it as an enduring foundation upon which identity rests—is most conspicuously achieved each May when the group observes the anniversary of its founding. According to

Armstrong and Crage (2006), the commemoration of dramatic events is an important part of the formation of community and identity. Storytelling is performative; the act of telling and hearing a story links narrator and audience. Stories thus come to constitute an essential component of relationships and groups. "Whenever we talk we create a character for ourselves and a relation with others: We offer to constitute a community of a certain kind" (White 1990, xi).

The program of the St. Erasmus VOTF anniversary meeting serves to institutionalize the shock they felt in 2002 by embedding the event in the yearly schedule. The heat of the original cognitions becomes tempered by a turn to ritual solidarity. It also offers an opportunity to retell the events to those who might not have experienced them firsthand, incorporating those who were not present at the beginning into the collective memory of the group. Moreover, as an enacted narrative, the anniversary meeting resolves the second problem of some emotion: its unruliness. At these yearly meetings the scandal is rehearsed, the sense of shock expressed, but there is another element. By the time we began our observations an appearance by the pastor of St. Erasmus to accept a donation from the members of the group to the parish in gratitude for allowing them to meet in the church hall had become regularized.[17] The ceremony is ostensibly to express the group's gratitude for being allowed to meet in the church. But it also provides a chance for the pastor to say thank you and to praise the group for its work, validating the members' standing in the parish and as Catholics in general. On multiple such occasions Father Francis called the group the "conscience of the Church"; thus, as an enacted narrative, the commemoration resolves the dilemma by dramatizing both the betrayal and the reconciliation.

As they told it, the VOTF origin myth is a story of the loss of innocence and of marginalization. It offers dialogic and temporal accounts of personal and collective identities, counterpoising their current activist selves with past quiescent ones. Whereas before the scandal VOTFers described themselves as experiencing a unity of faith, practice, and identity, after the scandal they felt the pain of division, opposition, and troubling alienation. The allegiance to faith, institution, and hierarchy that was generally an unproblematic foundation for their identities as faithful Catholics was suddenly dilemmic. Following Giddens and Jasper, the sexual abuse crisis and the events following its revelation were critical episodes that threatened the ontological security of these VOTFers.

With time and experience, members of St. Erasmus VOTF developed a repertoire of stories that reconstituted them—individually and collectively—as faithful Catholics *and* as challengers. What they experienced as a moral imperative to respond to the sexual abuse scandal endangered their ability to tell their autobiographical and communal stories of the Church or of themselves as faithful Catholics. Yet even as it imperiled many of the familiar stories that were fundamental to the VOTF members' narrative identities as "faithful Catholics," it opened up possibilities for new storytelling and the reconstitution of a new collective identity. The narrative challenge facing St. Erasmus VOTF continued after fashioning stories of their initial involvement. Subsequent stories were crafted and told to interpret and explain their continued activism. Since origin narratives provide a foundational emplotment and thus a key source of identity, frequently challengers anchor themselves in the initial working plotline, even as they are confronted with changes of fortune and circumstance (Owens 2008, 28, 91; Nepstad 2001, 32). The origin stories of shock and of being "pushed" got them going; their belief that their efforts would be welcome and effective sustained their early effort; but those stories that linked their past with their present and future furnished them with a measure of coherence and thus a basis for their emerging identity as activists.

Successor Stories: Steps on the Path of Progress

The origin story endured as a touchstone for the collective identity of the group years after it coalesced. However, as time passed the group developed successor stories to provide its members with a continuing sense of traction along a path. Whereas the origin story emphasized being swept up into participation, successor stories highlighted agency and willful perseverance. These stories shifted the sense of temporality by projecting a more recent present into a future and thus fashioning a continuity. They also offered an underlying message that the group could not afford complacency and that there was still resistance to be overcome. The horizon was partly illuminated by success in the present, but the group needed to remain attentive to its changing shape.

Many members explained that the pressure exerted by the Boston-area VOTF partly had prompted a series of reforms from a foot-dragging archdiocese. Chief among these was the transparency of the archdiocese's financial records over the previous several years. In her reflections on the accomplishments of VOTF, Victoria observed:

Okay. I think a lot. A lot. One, the financial records of the Archdiocese of Boston have been published for three consecutive years. The first year there were copies available in all the churches. Well, that's not true—there were copies available in my church and they were supposed to be available in all the churches. But that does not mean they were put in all of them—that is a biggie.

Sarah echoed Victoria's account of the organization's achievements: "Yeah. I have come to believe that the existence of Voice of the Faithful is and has had an impact. Now, specifically? I would say that—I don't know when it was. It's not very long ago. What, three or four years ago that the archdiocese decided to publish its financial statements? I think that's pretty connected to Voice of the Faithful." Ralph Mazzarella similarly noted that "I think locally, in the archdiocese, it's had an effect. That's where the major effect has been. . . . Now the archdiocese has come up and had to show their finances."

Relatedly, St. Erasmus VOTFers provided accounts of how VOTF presence and activism had empowered local parish councils, bolstering the voices of the laity in local governance. This was interpreted as an important structural change writ small. These accounts offered the realization of voice in Church affairs and suggested the possibility of greater lay participation in the future. As Phil remarked, expanding on financial reform, "I think that some of the financial stuff has gotten better . . . and it seems like parish councils have taken on a better role. So I think they've been empowered from a distance." In a September 2008 retrospective discussion on successes in the push for structural change, both of these accounts of financial transparency and the strengthening of parish councils received pride of place.

An important dimension of many of these success stories is the way in which they recognized that the VOTF achievements largely would go *un*acknowledged by those noninvolved or hostile to the organization, particularly by the hierarchy. Mostly they emphasized how gaining traction had been and would be realized through self-reflexivity. As a national activist for structural change noted at one meeting in the late fall of 2007, "the Boston area had achieved significant results with the first financial report last year that was 'very good.' The archdiocese will never give the VOTF any credit. It's important for everyone to stay vigilant: Accountability only works when we all do our part." In discussing the achievements of structural change in the September 2008 meeting, Shirley mentioned the reform of the priests' retirement fund: "We weren't mentioned but you know we were a force. We recognize that this is one of our major efforts. It was unfortunate that VOTF was not mentioned, but the VOTF has been responsible for quite a few things." In discussing VOTF's accomplishments, Ralph likewise noted, "I think maybe the cardinal listens to us more. Although it isn't—it doesn't seem obvious, but I think he's there listening."

Another story that members relayed centered on community. Recall from the prologue that most members of the St. Erasmus chapter did not personally know one another, and that they went to the initial listening sessions largely as unconnected individuals. Six years later, many told a story of emergent community building. Where in the past they had been relative strangers, now they had a sense of cohesiveness by which they could envision continuing into the future. At the sixth anniversary meeting of the chapter, for example, Peter recounted how St. Erasmus VOTF had developed a sense of community not often found in the Catholic Church. At a January 2009 meeting commemorating the revelations in the *Globe*, Thomas reflected upon how the group had developed into a "life-giving community." Successive planning meetings in other years also featured some version of this narrative.

Partly the story of community captured a growing sense of interpersonal attachment. As Ralph reflected on his continued participation in the chapter:

I think we just decided to go and there were, you know, other people from other parishes that I did not know. But as I got to know the people, you know, I think it was—it was more like a camaraderie. Getting to know the people and realizing how talented many of [them] are. Surprisingly. It was good. And I felt that I should continue because I felt an obligation to do so and to go just about every week. . . . And mainly because I should continue to go to the meetings, because if I didn't I would be disappointing those that are still going.

For some, this story encompassed the enrichment of their faith as well as their personal ties. As Joe reflected, "It's built up quite a prayer community here. . . . So I can't really point to this group except to build up a great community and everything. Very prayerful, thoughtful community." Similarly, Phil and others provided accounts of a prayerful community in which they were fully realizing their status as "adult baptized Catholics." Incorporated into this narrative are the necessities and pleasures of members' continuing education as faithful Catholics that the group provided them. Reflecting on the number of speakers the group had invited, one member said, "We have to learn and we have to know more, and that's the only way we can make changes: by knowing more." As Phil noted at a planning meeting, over the first decade they had brought in many speakers and "studied like crazy" to understand their role in the institutional Church and to deepen faith sharing. Father

Francis shared this storyline: "Before they started they were more theo-logically sophisticated [than other parishioners] and I think it's only increased with the education that they've gotten over the years, with some frequency."

These successor stories, as Polletta has emphasized, have ellipses: They invite more storytelling in similar veins and work against a sense of closure and finality. They have an open-endedness, keeping narration in motion in an emergentist sense. Successor stories offered a shared understanding of both continuity and evolution but, significantly, not stagnation.

In origin stories, time collapses or contracts: Something must be done *now* in order to alleviate the crisis. Subsequent stories are constructed within an expanded temporal horizon in which the group locates it-self and its work in the relatively distant future. Whereas in 2002 many VOTFers thought they would be done in a few years, by 2006 the group began to raise the idea of a fifty- or one-hundred-year plan. Referring to this difference, Victoria observed at one meeting, "The shock and hor-ror have gone and here we are plodding on and plodding on." To which Phil responded, "It's not easy being durable."

What helped them to continue plodding on and on was their abil-ity to project themselves into a "future perfect" tense, a point at which time, having at least partially realized their goals, they would leave a lasting legacy to others. At one of St. Erasmus VOTF's anniversary meet-ings, Jim Post, a former president of the national VOTF, alluded to this legacy: Members would not see all the changes in their lifetime, but it was apparent that they had created cracks in the foundations.

At one level, the idea that they would not see change in their lifetime could be dispiriting. But it seemed to have a different effect on St. Erasmus VOTF. Albert O. Hirschman considers this counterintuitive effect of piece-meal success "intermediate outcomes and halfway houses," as he puts it.

But this dissatisfaction is not in itself a reason why one would necessarily expect a turning away from such action on the part of any but the most naive and weak-willed public citizens. . . . In the case of public action, the partial and incomplete nature of the outcome can be interpreted not only as disappointing, but as encouraging. The fact that there is unfinished business left over after every advance could well reenlist the energies of our public citizens and thereby stave off the point in time at which they would want to give higher priority than before to their private pursuits (1982, 95–96).

Ironically, then, the receding temporal horizon shifted the atten-tion of St. Erasmus VOTF from future outcomes to the present in which they could realize their potential by showing up and persisting. As Barb noted, "We know what we want. We're not searching as we were in the beginning. We know what we want and we're going to continue to work on it until we get there. And the people that are now involved will stay as long as they possibly can. Until they can't manage to drive out there every Monday." Phil echoed this sentiment when he said, "I don't tend, in my own life, to focus on outcomes. I tend to focus on the process and the people I'm with."

These successor stories served as a bridge from the rupture recounted in the origin story to a sense of ongoing agency for the long haul. To make sense of their collective identity and challenge, however, they also needed stories that served as bridges to their pasts, stories that narrated the time before the origin.

Before the Origin

"And below is always the accumulated past, which vanishes but does not vanish, which perishes and remains."
MARILYNNE ROBINSON, *HOUSEKEEPING*

In defining the beginning, origin stories entail the strategic "forgetting" of events that preceded it. By narratively creating a moment that cleaves present from past, they offer the possibility of a new identity, both individual and collective. But identity is also constructed by selectively "remembering" a past that connects—or accounts for—the "before and after" of the origin. "Beginnings," according to David Scott, "[mark a difference but] are also recursive, conserving, connecting to the pasts from which they take their leave and measure their distance" (Scott 2009, vii). In order to claim an identity in the present, the members of VOTF had to narrate a past that offered an account of how they got there. In a sense, the origin story is a history of the present that backfills the narration of current action.

Much like the origin and successor stories, these too have a place on the shelf of the inner library of narratives. They are often templates that provide a sense of ontological continuity and offer moral guidance and lessons learned. They are like temporal maps constructed in the past that make sense of future possibilities for action. As Arthur Frank notes,

People's belief that an act is the right thing to do, at minimum acceptable and at most ethical, is embedded in stories they learned years before, as those stories have been adapted through the narrative trajectory of repeated telling. Few of these stories may be actively recalled; they are mostly a tacit resource. (2012, 157)

Many of the stories the members of VOTF told about their pasts involve enduring lessons about equity and justice and standing up to abuses of power. Although the stories were often about clerical abuses of power and privilege, none was about sexual abuse. The specific injustices, we argue, are less important than their responses to them. These stories stand in stark contrast to the claims of being passive, obedient, and naive. By excavating a past in which members refused to remain silent in the face of injustice, these accounts offered a warrant for their challenge to the Church.

These stories also have a generational basis. Nancy Whittier (1995, 1996) has emphasized how generations bring their specific understandings to social movements over time, coloring movements with the stores of knowledge and practices of their time. Virtually every St. Erasmus VOTF member was from the same generation, and most spent their formative years locally, as we noted in the prologue. Their understandings of marginality, injustice, the institutional Church, faith, and community were forged in a set of largely shared experiences that gave them shape and hue.

Growing Up Catholic

In the case of St. Erasmus VOTF, the crisis triggered the retelling of a story of social marginality that these members and their families had told growing up in Boston Catholicism (as well as other regions). Most had come of age within the bounded solidarity of urban neighborhoods revolving around the parish. They attended local parochial schools, celebrated holidays with extended family, and worshipped at the local (often ethnic) church. Up until the mid-twentieth century, these Catholics, tied to an immigrant history, faced considerable anti-Catholic bias, both institutional and interpersonal. As James Carroll has written, "Such prejudice mostly took the form of an exquisite condescension, to the vibrations of which we Catholics were closely attuned" (2009, 43). These are autobiographical accounts rather than narratives of the group itself, but in sharing personal stories members constructed an understanding of how they already possessed the resilience to be challengers within.

One member we interviewed recalled being teased about having "dirt on her face" on Ash Wednesday; another told us that the twelve Catholic girls in her school were called "the Apostles" by the Protestant girls. One woman was excluded and teased for attending parochial school. As Margaret recollected,

I spent eight years at St. Mary's parochial school, but the neighborhood that I grew up in was mainly Protestant. The other kids said I went to a "Pinocchio" school. Once when I was in the Girl Scouts we were going to meet at a cabin on our bikes. I was told by my leader to meet the other girls along the way because I, of course, was not coming from the same school. When I got there one of the girls pulled me aside and asked, "Do you know where the cabin is?" And I thought that she was going to ask me to lead them. I said, "Well, yes, I do." And she said, "We want you to go by yourself." I was from the "Pinocchio" school. I was not part of the gang.

For many of the members of St. Erasmus VOTF, the only way to avoid such prejudice was to remain within Catholic enclaves, most notably the parish and the schools and neighborhoods it defined. Joe, a member of St. Erasmus VOTF, described the 1930s and 1940s as a "period of defensive Catholicism—'build the towers and keep the faith.'" As Thomas O'Connor (1998) observes, in these decades the archdiocese powerfully articulated that loyalty to the institution and its voice in city affairs was the way to overcome this marginality in the community. Participation in parish life and the institutional order of the Church, so the story went, was the only means of navigating such marginalization and ensuring a place in civic life. The parish was the seat and circumference of their lives.

In every parish, where church boundaries were as rigid and clearly defined as the ethnic neighborhoods in which those churches existed, parishioners followed a set pattern of religious devotions and traditional rituals that everyone knew by heart and that had few, if any, variations. Catholic churches were filled to overflowing at Masses on Sundays and Holy Days of Obligation, many parishioners attended early morning Mass regularly, and entire families would kneel down together to recite rosary every night before going to bed. First Friday devotions continued in every parish; retreats and novena attracted thousands of the faithful; first Holy Communions, Confirmations, and May Processions were an accepted part of community life in Catholic Boston. (O'Connor 1998, 234)

Within community and family there were also periodic reminders of these stiff lines of demarcation. Victoria recalled asking for permission to go to a Protestant wedding, while Florence asked and was denied permission to attend a dance at a Protestant church. Both the demands of the Church and the strictures of home and community signaled the denial of agency in matters of faith.

In the second half of the twentieth century, however, the social status of many Boston Catholics—including members of St. Erasmus VOTF—

was dramatically transformed. In the postwar period, they moved out of their urban enclaves into the more religiously and ethnically diverse suburbs.[18] As a group they experienced substantial social mobility educationally, economically, and professionally. Every one of the St. Erasmus VOTF members we interviewed had a college degree or higher; most were professionals and lived in affluent suburbs of Boston. Many of the core members of the St. Erasmus chapter were teachers, lawyers, engineers, and financial specialists, for example. Notably, the mobility they had achieved in civil society made them starkly aware of their relative powerlessness within the Church. When they spoke of marginality in the present, it was not within secular society, it was within the Church. At least for these VOTF members, an emerging sense of the laity as relatively powerless and overly compliant had come to supplant their sense of relative powerlessness in civil society. Rather than the Church buffering them from the slings and arrows of the larger society, it became the site of slights and exclusions.

However, the divisions recounted in these narrated pasts were not quite so simple. Woven through these accounts of growing up within the protective and paternalistic web of the parish are stories of what we call narratives of "quiet refusal." Despite frequent protestations about not being "joiners" or "rabble-rousers," or references to their (prior) lives as "pray, pay, and obey" Catholics, virtually everyone we interviewed offered an autobiographical story of taking a stand against injustice or the abuse of authority. In some cases, the individual was the one exercising moral autonomy and questioning authority. In other cases, the recollection was of a parent doing so and imparting an important early lesson. On one level, these stories of quiet refusal are not surprising. They are the recollections of persons who have committed more than a decade of their lives to standing up to the Church and calling for Church reform. One would expect a strong and long-standing sense of conscience and efficacy. Yet within the context of their origin stories—depicting their naiveté, passivity, and reluctance to get involved—the narratives of refusal seem anomalous and even contradictory. When asked to describe her life growing up as a Catholic, Shirley recalled,

If something happened in school where the discipline was kind of harsh, my parents wouldn't stand for it. My sister was treated really harshly one day. A nun slapped her. My mother was down there like *that*. And they knew never to do that again. They didn't say not to discipline us, but [they said], "Explain what's wrong. Let us know and, you know, discipline is fine, but don't hit."

Another member, Dottie O'Hearn, told a story of her mother dismissing the advice of a nun. When she was in seventh grade and about to be confirmed, Dottie was disciplined for talking in class, and the teacher called her mother in to school. Dottie's mother assured the nun that this would never happen again and mentioned that they were on their way to get a dress for Dottie's confirmation. The nun disapproved.

"You're having a dress made for her? And she doesn't know how to behave." And my mother said, "Well, we'll see." We got outside and I can remember crying in the car. And my mother said, "What are you crying for?" And I said, "Because I might not get my dress." And she said, "I just told that to the Sister." . . . [You get the picture] . . . if [my mother] didn't like the way a particular priest talked, she'd speak her mind.

Some of these stories of refusal were more recent, and the refusals were not necessarily silent. Margaret Scanlon recalled an experience she had years before when she was attending Mass on Cape Cod where she and her husband had a summer home.

There was this young priest and all he talked about were little boys. It never occurred to me to think anything about it at the time. But one day after Mass I said, "Father, do you realize that half of the church population are women? And you never talk about anything but little boys?" So the next Sunday he gives his homily and on the way out he said, "Mrs. Scanlon, was that okay?"

Margaret assured us that "I don't hold priests on a pedestal at all." And, "I certainly was very willing to criticize priests."

Loretta Patillo is one of the more conservative members of VOTF, particularly regarding structural change. For years, she was a member of the parish council at St. Erasmus and active in various parish activities. Yet she recollected a time when she confronted the former pastor of St. Erasmus for what she saw as an arbitrary use of his authority.

We had a nun who was a pastoral assistant who worked with the sick and the bereaved and so forth. And she was at all the Masses every weekend to talk to people to find out how everybody in the family was and did anybody need anything. Everybody loved her. I think he was very jealous of the attention that she was getting. So he banned her from the Masses. So I spoke to him about that. I said, "She needs to be there because that's how she finds out who's going to need her help." . . . He ultimately relented. But the fact that I stood up to him was, you know, all downhill from there.[19]

Reflecting on her childhood, Bridget recounted a story that seemed to sum up the influence of her early family life and the direction of her future faith, feminism, and politics. She recalled a time in the 1930s when the downstairs tenants sublet their apartment for the summer to a family visiting from Washington, DC.

> When they finished looking at [the apartment] they said yes, they wanted to take it. Then the woman asked my mother, "Is there a rooming house in town?" And my mother said, "No. Not that I know of. Why?" And she said, "Because we have a n——— lady and we want to find a place for her to stay." And my mother said, "Well, I'll rearrange my children and she can stay with us." The woman said, "You didn't understand me. She is a n———." And my mother said, "I did understand you."

The woman worked for the family downstairs but lived with Bridget's family that summer and became a friend of her mother. "It was great that my mother had another woman to speak to. We had a screened-in porch with an awning. And when Lucia finished her work and my mother wasn't nursing the baby, they talked. . . . You know, you wonder the places where you get positive influences."

What is most remarkable about these stories is that almost everyone offered one unsolicited; we never asked about an earlier time that they had stood up to or questioned authority. The stories of quiet refusal were not only common but similar in many ways. They all feature some measure of principled defiance in the face of a perceived injustice or exercise of arbitrary authority. What is most remarkable about the recollected events, though, is how unremarkable they are. In the context of the sexual abuse and cover-up, the injustices and overreachings that are recounted in these stories are not extreme or egregious: a harsh and judgmental nun, or an egotistical and dictatorial priest. Indeed, for their time and place—Catholic parishes and schools in early-twentieth-century Boston—these incidents were no doubt commonplace. In fact, the familiarity of the conflicts suggests that these stories are less about plot than they are about character: The refusals to accept or comply with authority are evidence of an independence of conscience belied by their self-characterization as passive, "pew" Catholics. In short, these stories provide an autobiographical counterweight to their stories of obedient and blind passivity and a prologue to their current involvement with VOTF. In some ways they demonstrate that these VOTFers knew the emplotment of resistance in ways that did not depend on "hot" cognitions. They are submerged templates that could be drawn upon by these challengers within to craft both their origin story and successor stories that narrate their agency against inequity and authoritarian fiat.

Conclusion

From an emergentist perspective, storytelling is a recombinant activity that occurs as people rework narratives from their repertoire within the limits of available institutional scripts. Building on Owens and Polletta, we argue that challengers get traction for mobilization and contention through origin stories. These stories typically downplay challenger agency and highlight the compulsion for action. When St. Erasmus VOTFers offer their narrative of mobilization, they emphasize forcefully being swept up into the maelstrom of response to the revelations of the abuse crisis. The pressure to respond overcame their reluctance to participate because an institution that anchored their lives was imperiled. Tellings of the origin story generally contained some version of the mantra *never again*, which projected vigilance, and therefore continued activity, into the future. However, in and of itself, recitals of this narrative could not provide all of the traction necessary to keep the group in motion. The ritual recitation of origin stories can turn traction into an impediment to movement, the dilemma of being stuck with and in a past increasingly less able to envision possible futures.

Successor stories were necessary to provide a sense of collective and individual agency and to weave the past, present, and future together in dynamic ways. Members drew upon a small stock of shared narratives that elucidated concrete gains, even in the face of nonrecognition. They also provided a prospective orientation by reanimating the VOTF project to "Keep the Faith, Change the Church."

The individual stories that end this chapter became salient in terms of squaring members' deeply held identity of being faithful Catholics with their present and their challenges to the hierarchy. To provide some sense of ontological continuity they resuscitated narratives of challenge and agency from their youth. Even in an age when the laity was wholly quiescent and the hierarchy reigned unquestioned, their parents provided models of going against the grain. As personifications of being faithful Catholics, these parental lessons provided a history to be reclaimed when members self-reflexively explained and examined their own activism. They too helped overcome a dilemma.

Temporality is a key axis in the emergent process of collective identity, but their relationships with those individuals and groups outside of the VOTF and eventually relationships within the chapter also presented challenges to the affiliate. As we move to these two axes in the chapters that follow, we encourage readers to remain alert to how some of the stories we examine have shifts in temporality and messages of continuity that we have analyzed in this chapter.

THREE

Narrating Self and Others: External Relational Axis

The initial challenge for VOTF members in forging a collective identity was to establish a narrative arc that would meaningfully reconcile their pasts with their current activism and the Church's history with its future. Although stories of their past and future continued to be told, almost immediately the group faced a new identity challenge. During these early years, the members of St. Erasmus VOTF found themselves the object of criticism and censure by others. For some, including some lay Catholics and some members of the clergy and Church hierarchy, the members of VOTF were seen as troublemakers: insiders who were "scandalizing" the faith by keeping the abuse and cover-up alive. Paradoxically, to others, especially some survivors of clergy sexual abuse and those who were skeptical of the possibilities of reform or change, the members of St. Erasmus VOTF were too committed to the Church. Many survivors asked the same question from an entirely different position: "How could you remain faithful to such a flawed and corrupt institution?"

Barb Kelly, a single professional woman in her early sixties, echoed the sentiments of almost the entire membership of St. Erasmus VOTF when describing her initial reaction to the revelations of sex abuse and cover-up: She was horrified, enraged, and felt that "something had to be done." She was also typical in that—despite her anger and repulsion—she never considered leaving the Church. Barb had only recently returned to the Church after thirty years of having lapsed in her practice, although not in her faith. Deciding to return, she became an active member of the parish, working in the food pantry, serving as a Eucharistic minister, being a greeter at Mass, and volunteering to visit sick parish members. Her answer to the question about remaining in the Church after the abuse and cover-up was made public was emphatic. Having just reembraced her Catholic practice, she was adamant: "I'm back. I'm not leaving."

Her decision to stay within the Church and join VOTF meant that she—like almost all of the VOTFers—was cast as an outsider by some members of the Church. Of the three goals, Barb was most active in supporting survivors, the goal that, at least initially, entailed the most public and controversial forms of challenge. Supporting survivors often involved very public forms of challenge, such as picketing or protesting outside of—and sometimes inside—churches. Although all members of St. Erasmus VOTF were questioned and criticized for their involvement in the group, the public protests exposed VOTF activists to particularly intense censure from others. Barb recounted a time when the local police were called when, in their role as communicants, a small contingent of VOTF members silently protested during a Mass.

This past winter I went up to Maine. They were picketing because the bishop wouldn't talk to a woman about her son's situation. [S]he was the Eucharistic minister [in the parish]. He had her removed. He had her removed from all activity within her parish. And she just wanted to say, "Why didn't you do something about the situation when you knew my son was being abused years ago?" He wouldn't talk to her. So we went up there. We didn't picket this church. We went inside and we went to Mass. The bishop was saying Mass there that day. And we wore signs that just said, "Why won't you talk to Mrs. X?" We wore them right on our shirts and we went up to Communion. He called the police. And they saw that there was nothing going on and they turned around and left.

Her efforts have drawn criticism from friends and family, as well.

One time a number of years ago I was picketing a church in New Hampshire against McCormick. Cold day, let me tell you. And they wouldn't let you in the church. The Protestant church down the street did. It was very cold out. I called my nephew who lived nearby. And he said, "What are you doing up here?" And so I said, "Are you going to invite me for coffee?" I told him what I was doing. And he said, "No. I'm not inviting you for coffee." And he hung up. This is my godchild. He's very involved in the Church, Knights of Columbus—does all these things. He's on the board that has to do with closing the churches up there. He's very involved in the Church. He said, "I would never say anything against any of the priests." And I said, "And your two children are altar servers, right?" And he said, "Yes." So I emailed his wife a list of all the priests in the area that they should watch out for around my great-niece and -nephew. And we get along fine since, but we can never talk about religion.

Ironically, neither could Barb talk easily about religion with the survivors on whose behalf she protested. Many survivors of clergy sex abuse feel betrayed not only by the Church but by rank-and-file Catholics for not responding powerfully enough to the abuses of sex and power. The survivors' sense of betrayal makes it difficult for members of VOTF to speak openly to survivors about their own faith and loyalty, about being "insiders." One active supporter of survivors, a core member of St. Erasmus VOTF, said that he cannot reveal to survivors that he is a committed practicing Catholic: "Nothing, nothing, no hints, no nothing, you can't mention God, prayer, Jesus, or sacraments or anything else. You can't mention that to them." The members of St. Erasmus VOTF must accept the rejection of the Catholic faith by the survivors while remaining silent about their own faith as a condition of their activism.

The precarious position of St. Erasmus VOTF in relation to the Church hierarchy, other Catholics, and survivors of abuse disturbs any simple distinction between in-group and out-group.[1] VOTF had fraught relationships with multiple constituencies, including Catholic laity who defended the Church hierarchy, clergy who were both criticized and supported by VOTF, and survivors of sexual abuse who, having largely abandoned the Church, were the outsiders on whose behalf VOTF often acted. There was, in other words, no single "other" or "outside" in relation to which they could define themselves or their project. The boundaries of the group were porous, multiple, and shifting, and the identity work the group engaged in reflected the predicament in which they found themselves. Even as they were drawing boundaries that defined their own group identity as faithful activists, they were running headlong into boundaries drawn by others to deny them standing as good Catholics. Much of their early identity work consisted of negotiating the tension between differentiation and inclusion. In her study of feminists within the military and the Church, Mary Fainsod Katzenstein wrote, "A distinction between inside and outside needs to be made, but these locations are at two ends of a continuum, and there is much shared space in between" (1998, 37). It was in this space that VOTF continually found themselves.

The Ban

One of the most significant manifestations of VOTF's marginalization within the Church was "the ban." A year after the founding of VOTF, the Archdiocese of Boston decreed that all chapters of VOTF formed after January 2003 were to be prohibited from using Church property as meeting spaces. Although St. Erasmus VOTF was grandfathered in, having formed before the cutoff date, the ban expressed the suspicion and hostility that the hierarchy had developed toward the organization. In many ways the ban spatialized the relational dilemma St. Erasmus VOTF faced. As one bishop in the Boston area wrote in issuing an early ban on VOTF meetings,

> The activities and promotion of the Voice of the Faithful must be curtailed in order to avoid further scandal and polarity among our parishioners. For the sake of unity and Catholic orthodoxy in the parish, it is inappropriate to foster these meetings and to allow the members of the Voice of the Faithful to meet with parish councils.[2]

The ban was a hot button issue for St. Erasmus VOTF. It symbolized the autocratic leadership of the hierarchy and expressed the Church's view of the VOTF as a dissident group, a characterization that they adamantly denied. Yet rather than dissuading them from their mission of changing the Church, the ban increased their resolve. A number of members of St. Erasmus VOTF mentioned that had they not formed their group prior to the ban, it would have been precisely what would have motivated them to join.

The controversy over the ban reminds us that an important, but often overlooked, aspect of collective identity work involves emplacement. Identities emerge not only over time, but also in material and symbolic places. "Territory," "turf," and, most conspicuously, the concept of "boundary" reference the constitutive capacity of place to illuminate identities. Place played a crucial role in VOTF negotiation of identity, because significant relationships with others that defined collective identity were place-anchored, particularly in parish spaces.[3] Access to the church basement offered what Mary Fainsod Katzenstein calls a "habitat," or a social and physical location where challengers within can gather and plan how to bring about change. In such places, groups can regularly come together to affirm their identity, voice their grievances, and strategize. Gary Fine calls such places "arenas," noting that "while numerous resources must be mobilized for group life, finding a place to gather is among the most essential" (2010, 362).

As habitats, places define the group by offering a site or back region for composing the "inside." It is in these arenas that groups withdraw in order tell their stories, plan, engage in ritual practices, socialize, and generally forge a sense of purpose and identity.[4] The church basement of St. Erasmus is such a resource. It is nondescript and generic. Indeed, there is no danger that a physical description of the basement where the VOTF chapter has met weekly for over a decade would betray any guarantee of confidentiality. The room is large, well maintained, and immaculate. Folding metal chairs are set up around roughly fifteen tables on worn but polished linoleum. There is a slightly raised stage in the front. The basement is hot and muggy in the summer and cool in the winter. The acoustics are poor, the lighting fluorescent. In the back is a stainless steel, industrial-type kitchen with a pass-through into the room. Except for a crucifix and a picture of Jesus, the room is surprisingly secular and un-adorned. Ten years after the group started meeting there the room was totally redecorated with paint, new drapes and flooring, air conditioning, and an elevator from the first floor. But these physical refinements did not change the importance of the room to St. Erasmus members. This is be-cause the room's value is not principally material but social and symbolic.

First, the coordinates of the space within the walls of the church signal the VOTF's insider status and thus their right to "inhabit" the church. Even more than physical places where plans can be made and actions can be coordinated, such habitats carry their own history and culture. They are, thus, capable of bestowing meaning on their inhabitants and their actions. In this case, the symbolic import of meeting weekly in the church basement was not lost on either the hierarchy, who eventually banned the practice for later-forming chapters, or the members of St. Erasmus VOTF, who acknowledged its symbolic value. As one regular attendee noted, "And I think meeting in the church is very—it's a good thing, because we're in the church. If you meet outside the church and you think you're trying to change the Church, but we're in it. It's right there."

Just as important, the space offered the opportunity for the group to regularly meet and express—through their mutual presence—that they remain intact, as if to announce to the world and to themselves: "*The group that last met here still exists.*" Habitats are containers that hold groups that are maintaining relationships across temporal and spatial absences. The group recognized and valued this function of the space. In explaining their persistence over the years, one member noted:

The other thing that was key was the meeting every Monday night. I think that's—that makes a difference. That's not to say that everybody ought to do that. But if you do that, something happens or doesn't happen in other ways, okay? So the result you see six years down the line is very much influenced by the fact of them meeting every Monday night.

As much as the basement hall, St. Erasmus parish was itself a kind of habitat. St. Erasmus was founded in the 1960s in an upwardly mobile suburb of Boston. The parish reflected the decade in which it was established: modern, liberal, and young. The parish is situated within a comfortable residential area surrounded by a large, accessible parking lot. The building is redolent of the type of architecture so common for houses of worship built in this period. Through the doors one enters a plain but spacious vestibule. The nave is open and capacious, but not cavernous, with the pews arranged in a semicircle around a large marble altar. There is no physical separation of the sanctuary from the pews.

The nave and sanctuary reflected the spirit of Vatican II, what one sociologist has termed "the most significant example of institutional religious change since the Reformation" (Wilde 2007, 2).[5] The work of these councils (from 1962–65) called for the laity to take a more central and active role in Church affairs as the "people of God." Critically, Vatican II reimagined the Church as a community of members rather than primarily a hierarchical institution, offering a more collegial system of governance. These reforms invited participation and dialogue by the laity instead of quiescence and provided an institutional reflexivity through which their voices would be recognized. The councils also emphasized the conscience of its members as a faithful compass guiding their practice.[6] Vatican II proposed a new environment for participation, and within it the parish itself became a new habitat for spiritual and communal practices. The laity's transformed role was symbolically recognized in the reformed Mass. Prior to Vatican II the priest said Mass in Latin with his back to the congregation. The reforms turned the priest toward the congregants and Mass was said in the vernacular.

Many recalled how the energy and openness of St. Erasmus's early years reflected this shift. Grace noted, "It was like finding a home. It was in the post–Vatican II euphoria. It was swaying and dancing and what we called 'happy clapping.'" The first pastor, a beloved and charismatic priest named Father Ventus, openly invited the members to participate in the spiritual and communal life of the parish. Shirley noted, "There isn't a church like St. Erasmus," and she recollected her move from another Boston parish.

But when we went to St. Erasmus's it was—it was night and day. These people re-spected your intelligence. And they had good homilies that you could relate to. And you had plenty of discussion, open discussion. I have to say, all of these problems that we have with communication and all that we talked about with the hierarchy, we didn't find that in St. Erasmus's. It's a very open community. And part of the reason for that was that church opened right at the time of Vatican II. . . . Unfortunately, I wasn't there on the day it opened, but everybody talks about it. They said that Father Ventus stood in the front of the community and said, "This is my first parish and we have a lot of leeway. Let's talk about how it's going to be done."

Ralph, Shirley, and others recalled that during his homilies Father Ven-tus would solicit the congregation for their views on the issues he raised, a practice that could not have been done, or even envisioned, prior to Vatican II. Speaking about the first pastor of St. Erasmus, the current pas-tor, Father Francis, observed, "People just caught the contagion that he injected. They took pride in being progressive and being a little ahead of the curve." So significant was this parish history to the chapter that members from other parishes routinely referenced it as part of what makes St. Erasmus VOTF special. Some St. Erasmus VOTFers, such as Joe and his wife, recalled that they petitioned the archdiocese to move from their "dull" and "drab" parishes that were "in the dark ages" to be able to participate in this vibrant community. As Margaret observed in not-ing the character of St. Erasmus, "I would go to other parishes occasion-ally and I would say, 'Holy mackerel. What is this?' "

Over the years, the parish lost some of the early fervor and listed to the more conservative post–Vatican II Church. Despite this drift to-ward conservatism, when the sexual abuse scandal broke the pastor at the time actively encouraged parishioners to host listening sessions and later to form a chapter of VOTF. Many recall him climbing on the bus that would take them to the first national VOTF convention at the Bos-ton Hynes Auditorium in July in order to wish them well. "This is the most important thing you will ever do," he told them.

A Part of and Apart From

Despite the progressive history of the parish and the advantages of meeting weekly in the church basement, the group's regular physical presence within the church was also a source of constraint. Because St. Erasmus VOTF was granted continued access to the church basement at St. Erasmus, they were constantly reminded of the ways their project straddled the boundary of insider and outsider. Meeting in the church meant that they routinely confronted those who viewed them with wariness and suspicion, if not outright censure. Margaret remarked that many Catholics find Voice of the Faithful "an insult and not necessary." Ralph remembered a faith-sharing session organized by the pastor at St. Erasmus. During the course of the day's events, someone in the audience made a statement critical of VOTF and the room exploded in applause. Other parishioners took down announcements of VOTF events that were posted on church bulletin boards. The motives of VOTF members were questioned. A number of members recounted the antagonistic reception they received from the clergy, including Father Francis, who was installed as the new parish pastor about a year after the formation of the chapter. Members described him as more conservative and cautious than his predecessor. As Shirley told the story, "When Father Francis first came to the church he didn't want to hear from us. And, in fact, he had said to Peter one day, 'You're here on trial.' He said, 'If I don't like the way things are going, you're gone.' "

We vicariously experienced the precariousness of the VOTF's position in relation to the Church hierarchy. At the first annual picnic for priests of integrity that we attended Peter introduced us to a bishop. After explaining that we were sociologists interested in studying the group, the bishop asked us whether he "should call [his] lawyer." Although he was clearly joking, there was a hint of genuine wariness in the question.

But rather than drawing boundaries and insulating themselves from those who might question their loyalty, members of VOTF continued to work and worship in the midst of parish life, over time developing what one member called "thick skin." Most of them reported that rather than conceal or minimize their work in VOTF, they used their considerable parish service as opportunities to demonstrate their commitment to their faith. Among her many roles, Victoria worked with other members of her parish serving coffee after daily Mass.

I got to know a lot of people I hadn't known before. And so I talked about Voice of the Faithful. Some of them actively don't like it and they say things like, "Can't you just stop fussing about it and get on with things?" They say, "Well, that's over now." They say, "You're being disloyal to the Church." They say all sorts of things. But there I am and I'm pouring coffee and baking my special cranberry whatever, and they're coming around. They know now that I'm a person, not a devil.

Because Victoria and others remained centrally active in the parish these VOTFers interpreted and assessed their work from the perspective of other parishioners. Indeed, for a number of years, members of St. Erasmus VOTF experienced and expressed some ambivalence about their own activism. This fact became acutely apparent to us when, soon after we began attending the meetings, we naively referred to them as "dissidents." The word provoked a strong and negative response in a barrage of emails (of which we were informed but never read). They denied vehemently that they were dissenting and we quickly began using the phrase "change seekers" when referring to their activities in VOTF.

The relational and physical presence of St. Erasmus VOTF in the heart of the church signaled that the group was both *a part of* the Catholic community and, at the same time, *apart from* that same community. In the first few years, the dilemma they faced was to simultaneously mark group boundaries—in order to develop a collective identity—and to dissolve those boundaries, to be recognized and accepted as part of mainstream committed Catholics. Much of their identity work focused on managing this dilemma.

With this end in mind, the group worked to secure recognition and affirmation, especially from the clergy. Their first ally was Father Francis. Despite his initial wariness—expressed in his caution that the group was "on trial"—Father Francis became convinced of their loyalty and conviction. The group frequently mentioned how the pastor was quick to stand up for them when a local bishop suggested that he declare the chapter personae non gratae and advised the pastor to prohibit them from meeting on church property. Father Francis reportedly replied, "Those people from Voice of the Faithful are filling my pews. They're doing my lectors. They're serving Communion. They're taking care of my church. I'm not getting rid of them."

During those first three years the members of St. Erasmus VOTF also tried, unsuccessfully, to arrange a meeting with their auxiliary bishop. Diocesan priests, such as Father Francis, frequently interact with lay Catholics. They say weekly Mass and officiate at various sacramental rituals such as baptisms and weddings. They also engage with their parishioners in more mundane ways: dropping in on basketball games, attending church fairs, visiting the sick or bereaved. By contrast, bishops are members of the church hierarchy who rarely interact with lay Catholics in face-to-face routine interactions. Getting Bishop Ferrer to meet with the affiliate would be fairly unusual as a matter of course; the group's public stand over the sex abuse scandal made it all the more unlikely. Nonetheless, the group persisted in trying to arrange such a meeting. In fact, they saw it as more than simply a means to an end. Meeting with the bishop constituted an important goal in its own right. Grace remarked to us,

What we were looking for was a way to get the hierarchy to step down out of their ivory tower and communicate with the laity better. They're still not really doing it. But they know what we want. Because it's one thing that we keep saying. In fact, we did take a poll of everybody in the affiliate regarding what was the most compelling goal. And everybody said to talk face-to-face to the bishops. And you know we have a cardinal and we have four auxiliary bishops in the Archdiocese of Boston. And ours is Bishop Ferrer, and actually it took us four years. Three and half to four years, but we eventually did get a face-to-face meeting with Bishop Ferrer.

The bishop had been a mentor of Father Francis, and when the pastor agreed to facilitate the meeting, the bishop reluctantly agreed to meet with the group at the St. Erasmus rectory. When a member of the group who worked at the chancery approached the bishop to extend the invitation, he replied, indicating that he had been forewarned, "I know what you're going to ask me. All right. But this is it. I'll meet with six people. Not one more, or I'll walk out."

The account of this meeting is a successor story and a narrative staple of St. Erasmus VOTF. Uncannily similar versions were given in separate interviews we had with the people who attended. The meetings that occurred became collective lore, repeatedly referred to in informal conversations and large formal meetings. According to the often-told account, the informal dinner began tentatively with the conversation hovering in the realm of polite chat. As Shirley remembered,

So we had a little dinner. We prepared dinner and everything. And when we went for the meeting, he was already there. He was sitting down and there was a lot of small talk. Just about different things. And he and Father Francis knew each other from way back when, you know. And they talked about friends and things going on and so there's all kinds of jibber-jabber.

And Grace recalled, "He sat down at this dinner table and we talked about frivolities and God knows what else. His knee that was bothering him. The traffic . . . you know, all sorts of things." Finally, Peter broke the ice: "I know that you hear a lot about Voice of the Faithful. Well, tell us what you hear. We're not going to be able to talk to each other unless we know what's bothering you and you know what's bothering us."

At the end of the first meeting, Peter admitted to the bishop, "You know, we were really nervous to talk with you." To which the bishop replied, "Well, I have news for you. I was really nervous too. I really didn't want to be here. In all my years as a bishop, I never felt before like I was wearing a target on my chest." He went on to say, "I just felt like everybody was aiming at me. I never felt like I was so evil that everyone wanted to get me. I wasn't looking forward to this evening. But I have to say that I think you're good people and I think you're sincere. You know, I'd love to meet with you again. This was a really good meeting." When the group asked if he would be willing to mention his meeting to other bishops, he replied, "Well, I won't bring it up, but if they ask, I'll tell them."

The bishop did in fact meet with the group several times after that initial dinner. According to Shirley, who attended all of the meetings, "It was amazing. By the third meeting he was really genuinely glad to see us again. It was just extraordinary." At one point during the final meeting, "he went very quiet. He said he had been thinking of the El Salvadorian archbishop Óscar Romero, who had been assassinated."

"I've been thinking about Archbishop Óscar Romero recently. You know, he was a 'go along to get along' kind of priest and bishop originally. He didn't buck any of the injustice issues. He was sort of in tight with the government and everything. And he had an awakening as he got older and he thought, *I can't do this. I just can't keep quiet about the injustice that I see. And I can't keep quiet about the issues that need to be talked about.* And of course he got killed for it." And Bishop Ferrer said, "I was thinking about him. And thinking what a lot of courage it took to shift positions when you have a really comfortable life and everything is going just the way you want it to and then to step out of that comfort zone and be uncomfortable."[7]

The account of their interactions with Bishop Ferrer acquired the status of the proverbial "family story" told again and again to the same audience. In such stories, everyone knows what will happen and how. Indeed, the power of these tales lies in their familiarity: in both content and in the repeated act of telling, they establish identity and purpose. Like the origin story, this successor story too bears certain canonical features.[8]

The standard account begins with the bishop's refusal to meet with the group, a refusal that was overcome by the group's persistence, and their prior success in demonstrating their legitimate claim to being good Catholics to Father Francis. Most important, the three meetings encapsulate a triumphant trajectory for the group. The first meeting begins with "jibber-jabber" between the bishop and the priest, who are old friends. At that point, however, the asymmetrical lines of authority and status are leveled if not reversed. The tentative small talk with which the dinner began is called out by Peter in his open and frank invitation to talk and share concerns. And rather than VOTF "aiming" their outrage at the bishop as he feared, the St. Erasmus contingent admits to being nervous and elicits a similar confession from the bishop. The standard monologic interaction between hierarchy and lay—epitomized in the traditional confessional—is transformed into a dialogue. The VOTFers' success in persuading the bishop of their moral warrant to exist is signaled by his willingness to meet again. The series of meetings end, as the account relates, as far from small talk and jibber-jabber as one could imagine. The bishop reflects on the martyrdom of Óscar Romero and shares with the group the fact that he prays for the courage to put himself in the same uncomfortable position they occupy.

What is critical in this account is the focus on the relationships between the parties and the ways in which the bishop recognized the group members as "good people" and sincere. The story is important because it demonstrates that these St. Erasmus VOTFers had moved beyond passive, monological recognition to engaged dialogue with a Church authority. As heralded by Vatican II, everyone around the table was a member of the spiritual community exercising their conscience. What was being nurtured in the chapter meetings—respectful dialogue among equals for the vitality of the community—was realized around the dinner table. Through this dialogue the fading promise of Vatican II was being resurrected in the present in order to prefigure a transformed Church.

In the accounts of their encounters with the bishop it is never made clear what, if any, concessions he made, or if the exchange led to any changes in the role of the laity within the diocese. In fact, in all of the iterations we heard, it is not at all clear that the group presented any specific requests at all, except that the bishop share the experience with other bishops. In the way the story is constructed, though, and in the manner in which it is told, the group is granted what they sought from the bishop: a seat at the table. As such, in this context, they realized their identities as faithful Catholics whose voice and conscience were recognized.

In these stories of affirmation, other parishioners, the bishop, and the pastor not only recognize them as Catholics in good standing but eventually come to defend them against the criticism of others. The group's efforts to be recognized and for their standing as Catholics to be affirmed, particularly by those who were initially hostile and suspicious, continued to be a salient and important part of their identity. Their stories begin with a sense of division and difference and move to unity and identification. Of course, the dilemma of identity is that were they to give over entirely to the project of identification *with* other lay Catholics or the Catholic hierarchy—emphasizing the "sameness" end of the relational axis—they would not exist as a group or be in a position to pursue their goal of change. Thus, even as they claimed their membership within the Church and received confirmation of that membership from others, they needed to also assert their "apartness" by inflecting the difference end of the relational axis.

This and other stories that were repeatedly told and shared by the group demonstrate both the temporal and external relational dimensions of collective identity. Temporally, the story of the meeting marks a significant passage in the group's duration. Clearly, they see the bishop's engagement of the group as recognition by a member of the hierarchy, a key external other. In what we have noted as the continual movement of identity across sameness and difference, of continuity and rupture, this story is both ontological and strategic. It provides St. Erasmus VOTFers with an emplotment for their existence and moral authority, as well as a retort to naysayers and critics. It also demonstrates how collective identity is a dialogic process that emerges from interactions over time.[9]

Apart From: "We Are Not Sheep"

At the 2007 annual meeting of the national VOTF in Providence, Rhode Island, a button circulated among the attendees. It was a small round metal button reminiscent of political campaigns. The button depicted a drawing of a wide-eyed sheep bisected by a red line, the emphatic "not" of popular culture. The image is semiotically ambiguous. It makes fleeting reference to the Biblical metaphor of the flock, cared for by a loving shepherd. But it also alludes to a flock of sheep that are manipulated, en masse. It is the expression on the animal's face that privileges the second reference. In its wide-open eyes there is a knowing look of shock and disbelief; this is clearly not a *sheepish* sheep. As the St. Erasmus VOTFers reflected on the national conference at the meeting on the following Monday, they brought up the button and the words of a speaker who gave voice to its sentiments. "For the past two thousand years," she said, "we have been trained to be like sheep. *Baaa, baaa.*" There was general agreement striated with amusement and defiance. The button served as a symbol of their consciousness, agency, and willingness to act. In the middle of this discussion, Shirley casually mentioned that she watched a lot of cowboy movies. Puzzled by the apparent non sequitur, Phil asked, "Where is this going, Shirley?" With a bemused smile, she replied, "Sheep can stampede."

Shirley's mischievous reply was indicative of a larger shift in the group's collective identity on the external axis. Whereas earlier they avoided or downplayed differentiation as part of their identity work, by the time of the convention they came to embrace their difference from other faithful Catholics. They presented themselves as the conscience of the Church, as opposed to other silent, if not hostile, laity. Through this reformulation, St. Erasmus VOTFers pivoted in their relation to other laity and the hierarchy. They now recognized themselves as a leading voice of faith *and* participation. They had pursued a line from the VOTF prayer—"Help us to respect our voice and the voices of all the faithful"—and had found a new identity in this faithfulness as change agents.

Two or three years after the chapter began, St. Erasmus VOTF began a project of self-constitution, a project of "owning" a sense of Church history and doctrine. After a lifetime of subordination, they fully recognized both their previous quiescence and their individual and collective agency to be faithful Catholics apart from the expectations and commands of others.

With that end in sight, although the scandal and the struggles of the survivors continued to be on the group's agenda and the basis of many of its initiatives, meetings were increasingly dedicated to lectures, readings, and discussions about the Church and the role of the laity. As Joe remarked in an interview on changes over time, "I thought at the beginning it would be more definite action. But then . . . I saw it was kind of evolving . . . one characteristic being educating ourselves. Extremely important in so many areas." As a national activist on structural change commented, not only were they pursuing structural change, but also (with the apparent assent of the attendees), "We are changing the Church because we are changing ourselves."

The most significant component of their curriculum was Vatican II. As Michele Dillon notes, "Vatican II affirmed the values of equality, religious freedom, and diversity; recognized the importance of social movements in achieving change; emphasized culture as a human and social product; [and] validated the legitimacy of diverse interpretive stances" (1999, 48). Most of the members reported not appreciating Vatican II's implications for Church governance and liberalization at the time. As Victoria recounted,

So I do remember back and I do remember reading about that. But, I mean, most of—I think most of the council has actually happened. But I couldn't remember. I have sort of a memory of sitting on the train going to my evening classes and sort of reading about this. The council. It's sort of all tied with Buddy Holly dying and the things that were happening in my life. The big things.

This is not surprising given that most also claim that the early 1960s was a time in their lives when they were preoccupied with building careers and raising young children, and the council seemed like a remote event in their day-to-day existence. However, over three decades later, the sexual abuse scandal activated reclamation of Vatican II and the possibility of institutional and religious agency it had promised. They returned to the past for present validation.

St. Erasmus VOTF began expending considerable effort and time learning about and discussing the Vatican Council and other aspects of institutional history and doctrine. In the fall of 2007, three meetings were devoted to discussions centering on the changes wrought by Vatican II, with attention to *Lumen gentium* (the Dogmatic Constitution on the Church). There were also two lectures by local theologians on changes in priest formation and selection, as well as a talk by another theologian on the relevance of the Gospel of John to the VOTF project. In early 2008, an academic Church historian delivered a talk on the history of the election of bishops. In the early summer, two sessions were devoted to a discussion of a priest's reflections on the tragedies of September 11, 2001, and the revelations of January 2002, and a local Church historian presented a history of the democratic origins of US Catholicism.

These efforts represented the VOTF members' deliberate retrieval and reconstruction of an institutional past, and a deepening of their knowledge of the present to assert their independence from the hierarchy and stimulate their collective imagination of an uncertain and unfolding future. Vatican II in particular offered a model for the potential of collectively working together, even in the face of this uncertainty.[10] As Phil remarked to us, "But these [VOTF meetings] were all about people talking together and sharing ideas, which is the same thing that happened at Vatican II. You have all of these people and nobody knew exactly where it was going to go. Suddenly, by getting everybody in the room, *bingo*." Vatican II thus provided both a script for and a legitimation of their vision for the Church and their belonging as an empowered laity.

From day one, Vatican II was our shield. That's what we use as a defense for everything that we do and that's in our writings. It's in everything we do. We use the proclamations from Vatican II to say that it's our right. Pope John Paul II, you know, I think he has a hard time because he's old. But he kind of, he kind of swings around on the fence. Every once in a while he kind of, the light is there and he recognizes it and then he just, he shifts back. (Shirley)

This appropriation of Vatican II was one of many such efforts by St. Erasmus members to draw on Church history and Bible stories to consolidate their collective identity and use of the markers of legitimacy articulated by others to validate themselves. As Michele Dillon has noted, challengers rely "primarily upon Catholic doctrine to argue for the legitimacy of their identities and the construction of an inclusive and participative Church" (1999, 244). Sometimes these adoptions could take surprising turns. At a lecture in the fall of 2007, a theologian spoke on the meaning of the Gospel of John for VOTF. A key point of the talk was that every member of the Church was provided with the truth of the Holy Spirit, which can be used to interpret the present. "We are rooted in the past, but we live in the present," the speaker noted. A core member who was thoroughly enervated by what she had heard approached one of us directly after the meeting. Musing on the lecture and the subsequent discussion, she noted that she appreciated focusing on the Apostles. They were "just like us," she observed, since they made up the rules as they went along and had an important place for women in their religious practice. Her comments are not only a remarkable example of appropriation but also reveal a self-reflexivity on the group's process of emergence. They signaled a gendered consciousness that we saw repeatedly throughout our fieldwork, both among women and men, one that was expressed to both critique the hierarchy and advocate for the efficaciousness of women's voices in managing Church affairs.

This shift toward self-constitution also entailed an appropriation and negotiation of institutional practices and narratives through which the group enacted their status as faithful Catholics, both apart from and a part of the Church. St. Erasmus VOTF appropriated the idea of the parish (as in home), of the Sabbath (as in their weekly meetings), and of ritual (manifest in their prayers and songs that are fixtures of every meeting).[11] At one meeting a woman summed up the general sentiment: "[T]his is crazy in a certain sense, but Monday night is our Sabbath in some ways." In fact, the meetings resembled a religious service of sort. All meetings opened with the VOTF prayer and a hymn and concluded with the "Our Father" prayer.[12] The ritualistic parallels between Sabbath services and the weekly VOTF meetings were also evident during the first five years of the group as Peter exercised a pastoral authority.[13] Yet, even as Peter assumed the role of "pastor," in enacting the role he transformed it: never elevating himself above the group and remaining open to the voices of the "congregants."

Andrew Greeley asserted that the Catholic imagination is "liturgical," with stories and attendance tied together to produce spirituality (2000, 45).[14] More generally, stories of social relationships are "lived narratives" through which self and other are enacted (Gergen and Gergen 1997). If, as Ruth Braunstein observes with respect to religious storytelling, "The practice of telling and retelling . . . stories is akin to other rituals," then so too is the obverse (2012, 123). Narrative and ritual are intertwined in the construction of collective identity generally, and deeply so within this Catholic context.[15] The chapter developed its own ritualized calendar of events, including an earlier January meeting to recall the initial disclosures by the *Globe* in 2002, an annual picnic to support priests of integrity, and a celebratory anniversary meeting.

The annual priests' dinner became a way of both affirming and reconstituting the pastoral power of the clergy. The chapter and the local pastor invited priests who had supported VOTF during the earlier turbulent days, as well as clergy whom they recognized for their abiding service to their parishes. The mood was relaxed and festive. Members or their spouses grilled standard picnic fare and placed copious salads and other foods on a long table flanked by picnic benches. Members and priests casually mingled for most of the event with light discussion and sat at tables together sharing food and drink. At the very end of these events, Loretta or one of the other core members conducted a little ceremony and prayer in which the work of the priests was valorized, and each was presented with a small plant as a token of appreciation. Again, what was important here was the playing out of both sameness and difference, which simultaneously affirmed and transfigured pastoral power. The celebration confirmed the authority and integrity of the priests. At the same time that it restored the clergy to an honored position, the event, in its informality, was leveling, with priests and members circulating freely in friendly dialogue. Most importantly, in recognizing the contributions of the priests, the chapter implicitly demonstrated the role of lay Catholics to confer legitimacy.[16]

One of the more striking examples of the transfiguration of ritual was a meeting held in the early spring of 2008, both because of where it was held and who conducted it. This event was held in the church itself rather than the basement hall, and it was directed by Sister Bridget and a woman who was the spiritual education director from another parish. The woman was dressed in a white suit with black trim, the inverse of clerical garb. The event was billed as an exercise for spiritual reflection and all the attendees were female. The spiritual director first reviewed several songs that participants would be singing during the event and then asked the group to concentrate on a picture of Jesus washing Peter's feet. She asked those assembled to consider the message of the picture, and Grace, among others, suggested that it represented that everyone was a servant. The spiritual director led the group in a poem about the foot washing, followed by Sister Bridget reading the text John 13:1–15, in which the story appears. The spiritual director explained that the passage urged participants to receive rather than to give, since it focused on John accepting Jesus's love. They needed, she said, to let Jesus give to them. Letting themselves be loved is the bedrock of their own loving.

After the participants read and discussed the prayer "Christ's Attention," Sister Bridget observed that relationships were the heart of the group, which was its great contribution. Members had shared and reached out to one another over the last six years. Victoria said that she was struck by Peter's quick change of heart, at first rejecting Jesus's gesture and then accepting it wholeheartedly. This showed that God reached out to them to get them over their set ways. Shirley added that John was saying, "We are the Church." The event culminated in a handwashing ritual. A bowl and towels were set on the altar and each member approached, having her hands washed by the person in front of her and attending to those of her successor in turn as the spiritual director sang several songs. The meeting closed with a prayer led by her.

Woven through this ritualistic event was a woman-centered vision and practice of spirituality that drew on an institutional and traditional space and performance. In quiet reflection, communal dialogue, and ritual sharing, these women became the Church. As Leming (2006) and other scholars argue, this type of voice is a practice of articulating a new a religious identity within the confines of the institution.[17] It occurred within a sacred space in which the presence of male pastoral authority normally reigns, and had a spectral presence in its absence. For many of the women in the chapter, sameness and difference were realized in traditionally gendered divisions of Church doctrine and practice. Their participation in VOTF activities involved both the recognition and the transformation of these divisions. This ritual was not a version of Marianism, in which, through the veneration of the Madonna, the forbearance and purity of the female were exalted.[18] Nor was this ritual explicitly recognized as feminist. Indeed, a number of the women we interviewed during our fieldwork did not characterize themselves feminists, though they believed generally in women's equality and a greater role for women in the institutional Church. In the absence of any male authority, and through a shared practice of affirmation enacted in the symbolic handwashing exercise, these women produced an emergent identity as faithful Catholics in a strikingly female form in which they were both followers and leaders.

The boundary that encapsulated the St. Erasmus VOTF did not only differentiate the group from clergy or other Catholics; in time it distinguished them from the national VOTF. During the transition to a new president at the national level, the group found their sense of relationship with the national VOTF shifting so that they were themselves cast as the "other." In the fall of 2008, the new president came to a meeting to present his reorganization plan to move the national group forward at a time when it had experienced some contention about priorities and appeared to be losing members and momentum. The new leadership had produced a SWOT (strengths, weaknesses, opportunities, and threats) analysis employed by bureaucratic organizations and decided to create five new leadership teams around clusters of issues. These teams would coordinate more fully and closely with locals to both engage in more effective strategic planning and to present a clearer picture of VOTF to the public. As the president articulated the plan, brows furrowed and many in the group were visibly unsettled. At the end of his presentation, he encountered a number of skeptical questions, a few of which contained a slight tinge of hostility. The president seemed to be telling an unfamiliar story of VOTF's past and its future, one that did not align with the chapter's narratives of itself. Shirley and Grace were unclear as to how the new leadership teams differed from the old working groups. Others worried that the new model would factionalize affiliates and membership, as opposed to the St. Erasmus chapter, where all three of the signal planks were recognized and supported. A number of people expressed concern that the new model moved away from participatory consensus and toward hierarchy in which the national increasingly defined the locals' agenda. Barb too wondered how the national would know the locals' interests and concerns. Grace referenced Tip O'Neill, noting that "all politics is local." She suggested that newer affiliates were at a different point in their development than the established St. Erasmus. All of these anxious comments painted a troubling picture of distance and difference from the national strategy. One member later remarked to us, "I found that he wasn't speaking to me. It was—it was kind of like a mystery."

Prior to this meeting members of the national organization and other VOTF activists had called St. Erasmus—with its weekly meetings and many activities—a model for VOTF as a whole. Members also came to see themselves as an exemplar of the national organization and its praxis. The regular volunteer work by several members at the national office in Boston was a visible manifestation of this central role the group played. However, at the meeting in which the president laid out the new organizational structure, St. Erasmus sensed that they were being moved to the periphery of a much more rationalized, centralized, top-down organization. Their ongoing efforts, which had always been based on consensus, were being displaced by a hierarchical system of strategic planning, and worries arose about the impingement on their independence. From the view of these St. Erasmus VOTFers, they were becoming the "other" within their own organization.

The new national model never gained traction, and the St. Erasmus VOTFers' concerns receded. At the same time, this event and other controversies within the national organization led the chapter to define themselves increasingly as independent, charting courses of action based on the internal relations of the group and its members' concerns.

Conclusion

From their inception, members of St. Erasmus VOTF found themselves defining their identity as faithful Catholics and as change seekers in multiple relationships with others. This identity work was an ongoing effort not only to create boundaries but also, as often as not, to straddle them. In relation to those outside the local chapter, including the national VOTF, sameness and difference were mutable, dependent on the context of interactions and relationships with multiple others. St. Erasmus VOTFers narrated their collective and individual identities as both apart from and a part of other actors in the Catholic community, as well as those outside of it. Securing a sense of being faithful Catholics aiming to change the church paradoxically required this dynamic straddling. Initially other laity, many clergy, and the hierarchy cast them as pariahs, questioning their motives and their faith. While solidifying their identity as change seekers, and thus different from many in the Church, they simultaneously emphasized their sameness by continuing to actively participate in mainstream parish and Church life. As their sense of security on both sides of the sameness–difference axis strengthened, these challengers within became more secure in their project of change and their commitment to the Church.

While initially the group worked to overcome the condemnation of others and establish themselves as squarely a part of the Church, with time they began to recognize and value the ways they differed from others. Among the laity, they came to see themselves as the conscience of the Church. At one meeting during the Christmas season, the group read the Annunciation to the Blessed Virgin (Luke 1:34–35), in which Mary is told by Gabriel that she is to bear the Christ Child. One of the discussion questions following the reading was what they would take from the story. Grace commented that she felt that there were similarities with VOTF. The Holy Spirit was guiding them, she said, asking them to take on this burden and the scorn, derision, and insults from bishops and other parishioners. "I sometimes wish," she said, "I hadn't been asked."

In a parallel move, as the group grappled with its position within the Church, it reassessed its role within the national VOTF. This entailed the recognition of being somewhat different from the larger group. St. Erasmus VOTF came to sense its integrity as a group as emerging from its relationships with others, but increasingly in distinction from those same others.

FOUR

Narrating Multiplicity: Conflict and Coherence

Do I contradict myself?
Very well then I contradict myself,
(I am large, I contain multitudes.)
WALT WHITMAN, "SONG OF MYSELF"

Peter arrived early to the basement of St. Erasmus every Monday night in order to set up the card table on which he would put out name tags, reused copies of the opening prayer, a basket for donations, and, depending on the program that night, books, reprints, or discussion questions. As people trickled in he would greet them warmly and promptly call the meeting to order at 7:30 with the Voice of the Faithful prayer and a hymn, usually "Amazing Grace." Peter achieved this organization and routine without drawing attention to himself. He was quiet and pragmatic and, one sensed, deeply spiritual. Decades younger than many of the members, he did not so much lead the group as he sustained it. All members agreed that Peter's guiding dynamism was central to the first five years of the chapter.

Peter's humble and responsive leadership channeled the St. Erasmus chapter's energies and created a space for members to be heard and to coalesce. Much like the compelling force that pushed so many members to attend the early meetings, Peter's role as a leader was not the result of deliberation, forethought, or calculation. Rather, he arises very quickly within the drama of the early meetings to exercise a kind of pastoral guidance. Ralph started off the story by relating, "I don't know how Peter became the leader, but all of a sudden he seemed to be." A number of people told us that if they knew Peter at all before the scandal it was because he was a familiar face at Sunday Mass who had a regular spot in the pews.

Yet quite quickly Peter was orchestrating the group's energies. Members recalled him coming to the fore of the group in its infancy and becoming its key organizer in an unassuming way. Joe reminisced at a meeting that Peter had helped them solidify their sentiments that "this is our Church," and that he always "gave everyone a chance to contribute."

Phil similarly recollected Peter that had a "great gift":

I think the amazing thing about Erasmusans is Peter. He was incredibly hyper. I mean, he really was. But that was a great gift, because he was also extremely gifted at keeping six million things going. You know? . . . Or maybe he made me uncomfortable. I'm not sure. But, but it was wonderful. Because in his uncomfortableness, or what I consider uncomfortableness, he did not relent. . . . He wasn't afraid. Maybe he wasn't afraid of his own uncomfortableness. And that was a great model for everybody, okay? I mean, if he had been smooth and, you know, then other people, you know, would say, "Well, you know, Peter's got it all together and he's going to lead us. . . ." And he did. You didn't have that feeling at all, which was great. It was perfect. It was absolutely perfect. He was humble. He was not unopinionated, to say the least. I mean, he had strong opinions of many things. But he wasn't afraid to say them and let them be debated or something, okay? . . . The other thing that was key, I think—and he was very strong on this—was the meeting every Monday night. I think that's—that makes a difference.

Thomas echoed the sentiments of all of the members when he described Peter's remarkable capacities to maintain the momentum of the nascent chapter:

You have to recognize the talent that that man has. And he could just, he was the maestro. You know? He had the baton and he could keep the whole thing moving. You know, he didn't ruffle feathers. He didn't offend anybody. He got all of the ideas and he worked his butt off.

And he noted that Peter "didn't lead from the front" but rather "from the middle." He was "committed in the midst of a community of people who were committed." Thomas noted that he had an affinity for absorbing the commitments of others. He was a quintessential listener who took obstacles out of people's way and "let them do what they wanted to do." In this sense Peter was a master facilitator: "He gave each of us agency" and he "assisted the group in finding its own way."

Peter was never in charge, but he took charge of the many activities needed to sustain the group's energy and ambitions. He orchestrated the buzz of activity but also acted as a shepherd who sought to attend to each member of the flock. He exercised a strain of pastoral power that knit the members together.

The group's success during the first few years in managing the temporal and external relational dimensions of collective identity established St. Erasmus VOTF as an exemplar among national VOTF chapters. The group continued to meet every week. Attendance was stable and high. They offered a rich program of speakers, films, and educational events. They raised money for survivors, participated in public protests, and contributed money and time to the national VOTF organization.

By 2006, despite Peter's leadership, cleavages within St. Erasmus VOTF began to emerge. The factions mapped onto the three planks of the organization. Some members of the group started questioning which of the three goals should be the central mission of the organization. Even more than that, some members voiced concern that one or another of the goals was eclipsing the others. Rather than "planks" that scaffolded the work of the group, the three goals were becoming splinters that threatened to divide and, some feared, dissolve the group.

Conflict and Cohesion

Much of the scholarship on collective identity rightly emphasizes the integrative or "sameness" end of the internal relational axis. Groups strive to establish a sense of "we-ness" through commonality, shared values, norms, and purpose. They achieve this solidarity by engaging in ritual, finding a habitat, sharing common experiences, and narrating their mutual pasts, as the foundational work we earlier reviewed has emphasized.

When viewed from the vantage point of commonality and solidarity, the incipient conflicts among St. Erasmus VOTF would seem to signal the impending collapse or, at the very least, the paralysis of the group. However, the opposite pole of this axis, where difference, diversity, and even conflict emerge, is equally implicated in the construction of collective identity and group persistence, efficacy, and resilience. Despite the bad reputation of dissent and conflict in now classic studies of social movement groups—William Gamson (1990) refers to it as "a misery few challenging groups escape from"—Amin Ghaziani (2008) argues that what he calls "infighting" can be a resource for groups. He defines infighting as a particular type of conflict surrounding ideas about strategy and identity. Its dividends derive from the opportunity it offers for activists to engage in a metaconversation about who they are and what they should do, or about identity and strategy.

According to Georg Simmel, group conflict is a necessary—not merely a potentially beneficial—condition for group life. "[C]ontradiction and conflict not only precede . . . unity but are operative in it at every moment of its existence" (1955, 15). He claims that were a group to be totally "harmonious" or to achieve "a pure 'unification' (Vereinigung)," it would cease to exist as a group. In terms of our model of collective identity, Simmel's ideal type of complete convergence among members of a group would correspond to a situation in which the group had slid across the axis of variation to inhabit only the "sameness" pole. In such a case, the group's internal sense of itself as a group would lose the torque out which a sense of collective "we" emerges.

Kai Erikson makes a similar point about difference and diversity in his book *Everything in Its Path.*

[T]he identifying motifs of a culture are not just the core values to which people pay homage but also the lines of point and counterpoint along which they diverge. That is, the term "culture" refers not only to the customary ways in which a people induce conformity in behavior and outlook but the customary ways in which they *organize* diversity. (1976, 82; italics in original)

Whereas Simmel invokes the specter of total similarity (or unity) as the problem for groups and argues for the productive role of conflict for "group affiliation," Erikson suggests in this passage that variation or difference within a group is itself not a sufficient antidote to sameness. Diversity, he claims, must be *organized*, not simply present, in order to provide the counterpoint to similarity.

In what ways might dissent and conflict be said to be "organized"? One way is that conflict is a product or a manifestation of group culture or ethos as much as consensus or agreement is. Although conflict might appear to undermine the cohesion of a group, it may reflect higher-level agreements about what is valued and important. In other words, what defines a group is not exclusively what they share and agree upon, but those points of dissensus, or what they agree are "common points of concern."

Indeed, diversity may become a group value in its own right. Ghaziani claims that "infighting does not result in defection or dissolution in those cases where it comfortably facilitates a higher order consensus about 'who we are' and 'what we want.' . . . Infighting establishes what we fight about (diversity in our vision of identity and strategy) and how we fight (the rules of engagement and styles of deliberation)" (2008, 306).[1] In her examination of the German Autonomen, part of the "nondogmatic" German radical Left, Darcy Leach notes the group's explicit rejection of coherence and unity achieved through silencing, domination, or the elimination of dissent. For them autonomy is a central value that translates into a refusal to either be dominated or silenced or to dominate or silence others. This value presents a contradiction at the heart of their mission, much like the contradiction at the heart of liberal democracy itself: the balancing of community and conflict, the freedom to express oneself, to challenge, and to raise contentious issues on one hand; and the constraint inherent in the rules of engagement that requires tolerating the views of others even while refusing to allow them to intimidate or silence the other. These contradictions are not something to be eventually reconciled, however. Since they lie at the heart of their movement, they can only be provisionally negotiated and renegotiated consigning the group, if it is to persist, to "live in contradiction."

Leach's analysis also suggests that formal or abstract commitments to openness and dialogue might not be enough to organize emerging conflicts within groups and stave off the factionalization and dissolution so often associated with infighting. In order for cultural value of openness to actually pay dividends it must be embedded in what we earlier referred to as the friction and footing, or the "sticky materiality" of everyday life and interactions. Ghaziani refers to this concretization of culture as "resinous." By that he means that generalized and abstract values are attached to mundane logistical decisions. By putting these values and norms "to work," they become clarified, meaningful, and consequential.[2]

In this chapter we discuss how St. Erasmus VOTFers engaged in ongoing identity work along the internal relations axis to create unity within diversity. Their capacity to "organize" conflict, or "live in contradiction," was certainly not foregone. As we have described earlier, St. Erasmus VOTF did not bring to their activism a history, or even a commitment to the ideals of autonomy, conflict, or dialogue. As lifelong Catholics they were accustomed, at least in regard to matters of faith and religious practice, to receiving truths from the clergy. They began and continued to affirm doctrinal authority, even as they came to reject clerical authoritarianism. They were not used to hearing their fellow Catholics express dissenting opinion. It was not that as Catholics they were exempt from conflict or difference, but they were ill equipped to manage it, to organize it productively. Their success in eventually doing so suggests some conditions under which conflict and difference among a group can enhance rather than undermine the ongoing existence of the group.

The Emergence of Conflict

As we mentioned in the prologue, the early meetings at Wellesley and the listening sessions at St. Erasmus were, by most accounts, unlike anything any of the participants had experienced. These gatherings were sense-making efforts, to use Karl Weick's term; those who were present were facing a situation for which no story could yet to be told. They were heated and emotional. There was no protocol for how to manage or contain the intensity of the meetings. Looking back on those early meetings, people described them as "free-range" and "scattered." Margaret recalled an incident that suggests that they were, at times, combustible.

And I remember there was this fellow who is a member of Voice of the Faithful but also served on the archdiocese. And I remember him standing up and saying, "I want to caution us. That we're acting like we're at a football rally." And he said, "This is very difficult for me. Cardinal Law is a very good friend of mine. But I don't think this meeting deserves this kind of behavior." I mean, here are people my age acting [like] jerks. So it was a sobering realization that we were—were not at a football party and we're not at a lynching party, either.

The remarkably quick adoption of three planks became the bases for channeling these emotions and organizing work of both national and local chapters. Ironically, these working groups, with time, eventually became the source of emerging conflict within the St. Erasmus chapter. As members became affiliated and committed to one of the working groups over the other two, the differences in focus strained the overall unity of the chapter.[3]

The Needs of Survivors of Sexual Abuse

The smallest but most forthright of the working groups was strongly— and almost exclusively—committed to supporting the survivors of sexual abuse. The horrific abuse uncovered by the *Boston Globe* was, of course, the reason VOTF originally formed, and some members were convinced that it should remain the group's raison d'être. One of them, Florence, immediately gravitated to the working group dealing with survivor issues. "After hearing just one or two stories of the abuse of children, that what's really taken hold." For Florence the other two goals seemed of lesser importance. At the initial Boston convention in July 2002, Florence was deeply touched by a survivor who challenged the assembly to walk with survivors down to the Holy Name Cathedral, the spiritual home of the archdiocese, to participate in their weekly protests. For the next three years she found herself standing shoulder to shoulder with survivors and a few other allies: "I just had to be there."

With time Florence's participation in survivors' issues broadened and deepened. She became involved with Survivors First, a support group that started to compile a database of abusing priests and bishops who had covered up the abuse, and that worked on changing the statute of limitations for child abuse. She attended trials of the civil suits brought by survivors so that she could offer support and bear witness. She also joined Truth and Recognition, an organization dedicated to collecting the stories of survivors.

In defending the primacy of supporting survivors, Florence pointed out that if the stories of abuse had not come to light, there would be no discussion of structural change or supporting priests of integrity. Florence was open about the fact that her unwavering commitment to survivors put her at odds with others in VOTF, and particularly with the national organization. In the contentious 2008 VOTF election for the national board of trustees, a slate of candidates carrying the mantle on survivors' issues was pitted against another group that, in Florence's mind, wanted to shift the focus to structural change. Animosity lingered after the structural change slate won: "I feel like this structural change group just takes over and they want us to keep quiet."

While the structural change candidates were firmly dedicated to supporting the survivors, their commitment was not programmatic. When we asked Thomas, a leader in the group on survivors' concerns, how he would envision justice for the survivors of sexual abuse, he seemed to retreat from the word, even to the point of declaring that "there is no justice." Later he observed, "They will go to their grave with this burden," implying that there is nothing on this earth that can be done to make it right. Instead of speaking of justice, Thomas insisted that what is needed is "a response that is appropriate and adequate."

Thomas's use of the phrase "a response that is appropriate and adequate" expresses his conviction that justice for the survivors must begin and end with their needs and cannot be determined with any other goals in mind. The needs of the survivors cannot, in other words, be conflated with other ends such as ordaining women, empowering the laity, or other structural changes within the Church—regardless of how worthy or legitimate those other ends might be. "We are to care for these people. Now, caring for a person means you do what they need, not what makes you feel good."

Barb agreed. When we asked her how she perceived justice for the survivors, she responded:

You know, I can't answer that because *they* can't answer that. We've discussed, "What do they really want? What do they want from us? What can we do?" And they don't know really yet what they want. They just have to go day by day and we have to—If they say, "Do this for me," or "do that," you do it. If you can give them some money and that will help out, you give it. But I don't know what the answer to that is. Money is not the answer. These big settlements are not the answer.

By defining their mission in terms of the needs of the survivors, members of the Supporting Survivors group articulate a conception of justice that is yoked to Foucault's concept of pastoral power. From the point of view of the Supporting Survivors group, the systematic cover-up of sexual abuse on the part of the hierarchy constituted a massive failure of the Church's duty to exercise pastoral power. The Supporting Survivors group believed that the work of VOTF should be to step in and assume that ethic of care. As we discussed earlier, this did not mean that they tried to bring survivors, many of whom left the Catholic Church, back to the faith. It meant, instead, that the work of VOTF should be aligned with the needs of those who had been so grievously injured by the abusive priests and the callous hierarchy.

When we interviewed Father Francis he admitted that while he was initially cautious about allowing an affiliate of Voice of the Faithful at St. Erasmus, he has been persuaded of its significance. In particular, he realizes the primacy of supporting victims and appreciates that the VOTF keeps reminding them of the victims' plight.

As much as I might not want to see everything through the suffering and the injury done to the victims, it certainly has influenced me. In the [Catholic] Church we have this "preferential option for the poor." Where we need to see everything through the prism of the poor and [ask] "How does this decision affect the poor?" Now, do we always do that? No. It doesn't come close. But that is what we are supposed to be doing. So the VOTF kind of use that as a parallel and say, "Of those who have been abused, our obligation and responsibility is to them."

Despite their activism and commitment, members of the Supporting Survivors group often presented themselves as somewhat detached from the rest of St. Erasmus VOTF. There were a number of reasons for this positioning of the Supporting Survivors group on the margins. Like Florence, many of them were involved in multiple groups challenging the Church and working on behalf of survivors. They identified more strongly with the goal of supporting survivors than they did with any particular group or organization. Moreover, the nature of their activism differed starkly from that of the other two working groups. It was much more public and confrontational, often involving picketing Church events, attending rallies, and speaking publicly against the Church hierarchy. Other members of St. Erasmus VOTF privately would make allusions to the demeanor of the Survivors group, describing them as "strident" or "angry." Commenting on the members of the Supporting Survivors group, Phil admitted, "They are certainly very, very passionate and committed people and I think some people, some of us, can get turned off by the strength of their fury. It's a legitimate fury. But I think we have to find some way to, you know, kind of keep together about this."

Seeking Structural Change

While all members of St. Erasmus VOTF wanted to support survivors in some way, one contingent—whom we will refer to as the Structural Change group—believed that the leading goal of VOTF should be to fundamentally change the way the Church operates. Structural transformation, they reasoned, was necessary so that sexual and power abuses could not recur, but also for reasons unrelated to the sex abuse scandal. The Structural Change working group agreed with the Supporting Survivors group that the abuse of sex and power catalyzed lay Catholics to take action. At the same time, they understood the scandal in terms of centuries, if not millennia, of injustices within the Church. For those members who advocated for structural change, the real issue that VOTF should confront was one of power, exclusion, and secrecy. With appropriate reforms all those who had been silenced and excluded would find their rightful place within the Church: women, divorced Catholics, gay Catholics, and indeed all lay Catholics would be recognized and treated with dignity, autonomy, and respect. According to Shirley, a leader among this group, "[W]ithout structural change, you're not going to help anybody. You're not going to get to the root of the problem of why it was able to happen."

Whereas the Supporting Survivors group had a clear and unwavering sense of what they should be aiming for—responding to the needs of the survivors—the Structural Change group was less certain of the particulars of their path toward change. As we noted earlier, the overall project was embedded in the motto of the organization, "Keep the Faith, Change the Church." However, specific goals and a long-term strategy to achieve them were less apparent. At one meeting Shirley attempted to sum up the position on structural change by declaring that they were pushing for inclusion of the laity in nondoctrinal decisions to create a more positive sense of community. When we asked Shirley what specific changes would have prevented the abuse of power, she acknowledged that there was some disagreement even among those members of the Structural Change working group as to what changes were appropriate. The list was long and wide-ranging. The possibilities included abolishing mandatory celibacy for priests, ordaining women, increasing accountability in both Church finances and governance, and changing the Church's stance on divorce and homosexuality. At one point Shirley explained that the expansive list was in part a product of the early listening sessions, which became forums for airing general grievances about the Church: "People asked why or whether the church considers a divorce to be a greater evil than sexually molesting a child. 'Sexually molesting a child' became the counterpart to every other thing that irritated you about the Church."

For her part, Shirley based her sense of what changes would be appropriate on a distinction she drew between Church doctrine and "man-made" law. The latter could be questioned and changed. The former was, for Shirley, sacrosanct. Speaking about "crazy" man-made rules she said,

I wanted them to be exposed as being man-made rules, even though we as Catholics know that they're man-made. A lot of Catholics who go to Mass and sit in the pews don't really pay attention to why things are going on. They just accept it. That's just the way it is. Even when we formed, a lot of Catholics have a very negative view of us, because they think we're a schism in the Church. They don't realize that we're not doing anything that against the doctrine of the Church.

While many within St. Erasmus's Structural Change group agreed with this distinction, they were also acutely aware of going "too far" in advocating for changing even man-made rules. Speaking as individuals, many of them endorsed more far-reaching reforms than they officially or publicly supported as members of VOTF. Barb, who was affiliated with both the Supporting Survivors group and the Structural Change group, claimed she supported the abolition of mandatory celibacy for priests, arguing that the widespread sexual abuse would not have occurred had women been wives of priests.

Because I've often said and think . . . that if priests were married—which I think they should be, if they want to be married, let them be married—If there were women involved they would not have allowed this to happen. They would have seen these things going on and they, they just would not have allowed it. Maybe their husbands would be, but the women wouldn't be. And I don't think any woman could see a child being sexually abused and not say something about it.

Barb was also in favor of changing the role of women in the church more broadly.

When they say that women can't be priests, you think of Mother Teresa. You're saying Mother Teresa isn't good enough to say Mass? Are you kidding? Of course she was. It's not just for men. So I'd like to see more of women religious involved in the running of the Church.

But she was wary about officially seeking the ordination of women for fear of moving too fast.

But not yet. I think in time. But not yet. I think that would be too much. I think, let men get married. Let—let the entire Catholic Church see how women deal with the situation and then slowly, I think, women can be ordained. It has to be a little slower.

Ralph also personally supported many of the more controversial changes, at the same time that he conceded the need to "go slowly" out of respect for the beliefs of others. Reflecting on the original mission statement of VOTF, Ralph thought that it could have been worded more "diplomatically."

I think that [the structural change goal] was not worded correctly. I think essentially the structural change is hopefully to have a laity get involved and the priests and the bishops and so forth allow them to get involved. I think that's the intent of it. But I think it was too strongly worded. I think that put a lot of people off.

Differences within the Structural Change group seemed less pronounced because of the capaciousness of the concept itself and the aversion of VOTF to be programmatic from the very start. As a member of the national VOTF working group on structural change defined the phrase at a St. Erasmus meeting, "We would devote ourselves to advancing meaningful and active engagement of the laity in the life of the church."[4] As Ralph commented above, the structural changes that garnered the greatest widespread support were increasing lay involvement in the Church. In many ways this became the default definition of structural change that united the working group. Barb explained,

I think the structural change was always a problem group because people didn't understand what structural change meant. I thought it was very simple. I mean, you're not going to change the bricks on the building, nor are we going to change the teachings of the Church. We're just going to change the way priests and bishops are dealing with everything. We just want to get more involved.

Supporting Priests of Integrity

A third working group dedicated their efforts to supporting what they called "priests of integrity"—priests who were either innocent of any wrongdoing or who actually took public and risky stands demanding the resignation of Cardinal Law. The Supporting Priests working group wanted to shield innocent priests from the collateral stigma of the scandal, to clearly signal their appreciation of the continuing dedication of those pastors untainted by scandal, and to protect the rights of accused priests to a speedy and fair judgment.

They supported the diocesan priests by periodically inviting them to speak. They also hosted an annual picnic to recognize the work of priests of integrity within the Church and to offer the priests an opportunity to socialize with both laity and other priests. One of the earliest projects of this group was a survey of parish priests. The point of the survey was to describe the lives and concerns of parish priests and to hear in their own words what kind of support they needed. Sister Bridget described the survey.

So we designed—well, none of us was an expert on how to do it, but we designed a questionnaire that had three sets of questions. The first set of questions were kind of objective. Like, you know, are you a pastor or are you whatever? The second set of questions was about the scandal and about the abuse and everything, their dealing with their parishes. But then the third questions were my favorite questions, because [they were about] "What's going on inside of you? And what do you need?" And the first question of that set was, "This is the best of times and the worst of times in our Church. For you, personally, what is best? For you, what is the worst?"

The survey confirmed what many Catholics could observe firsthand within their own parishes. With a declining number of priests and the closing of parishes, the life of the parish priest was becoming increasingly lonely and difficult. It was no longer the case that three or four priests would live together in a rectory, sharing both their daily lives and the duties of a single parish, as had been the case throughout most of the twentieth century. More recently, a single priest would likely live alone and more and more frequently have to cover the clerical duties of more than one parish. The isolation of parish priests was exacerbated by the scandal. Priests reported feeling the distrust of some Catholics, even to the point that they would not wear their clerical collars in public.

In late 2008, a panel of parish priests from the area joined the regular Monday night meeting to talk about their experiences of the scandal. The program was billed as "Supporting Our Priests," and in introducing the panel Phil noted that the point of having the priests was to have a public conversation about how priests were being treated by the hierarchy, the laity, and other priests in the wake of the scandal. The first speaker offered a bleak picture of the life of a parish priest. He said that when the scandal hit, priests "hunkered down." It was, he continued, a time of "great isolation," a time when "our world fell apart." He reported that a significant number of priests suffered from PTSD.

A second speaker depicted a similar situation of being an object of distrust and becoming distrustful oneself. He mentioned that he felt ashamed to be a priest in public. People averted their eyes and even crossed the street when passing him. He recalled that before the scandal he would greet kids in the schoolyard and give them hugs, but after noticing the wary eyes of parents he stopped. All three of the priests reported, however, that the one place they did not feel stigmatized was within their parishes. Outsiders might view priests with suspicion and hostility, but the people in their parishes were "life affirming."

For the members of the Supporting Priests working group, these accounts and stories confirmed the need to work on behalf of priests. A number of those VOTF members who worked on the priest survey were surprised to discover that parish priests were not only isolated in performing their clerical duties, they were also relatively powerless in the Catholic hierarchy. In the course of interviewing a monsignor—a priest who has been recognized for his exemplary service to the Church—for the survey Margaret discovered that "in my lack of sophistication I thought priests had some power. But the monsignor said 'Absolutely not. Nothing. Zero. We get no say about anything.'" This realization seemed to create some sympathy for the priests who, like their parishioners, were excluded from participating in the governance of their faith.

Their concern for priests extended even to those who had been accused of perpetrating abuse. Several St. Erasmus VOTFers expressed a sense of injustice in regard to the indefinite wait that accused priests experienced while the Vatican decided their fates. With no clear timetable under ecclesiastical law for the resolution of these cases, those accused were stuck in a type of purgatory. The plight of accused priests awaiting some form of closure was seen as a case of the Catholic hierarchy exercising unbridled power in a way that clashed with more liberal and modern notions of due process and justice. It was also a clear abrogation of pastoral authority. One of the most active members, Loretta, bemoaned their circumstances, "hanging out there not resolved one way or another." At the event mentioned above, a panel of three priests who agreed to appear to discuss how the Catholic community could support its priests, the issue was raised several times. During the question-and-answer session Betsy observed that these priests need to be "healed" as well, and she characterized the removal and wait for one priest as "cruel." An attendee from another parish echoed Loretta's concern when he expressed that he hoped the accused would not be "hung out to dry." Rhonda followed soon after and voiced deep concern that a priest whose accuser had recanted had been "left in limbo." Finally, Ralph noted that he was praying for a priest whose case was unresolved. He considered the failure of the Church to resolve these accusations an injustice in its own right.

Grace participated in the Supporting Priests working group almost exclusively from the beginning. Although sympathetic to the plight of survivors, she believed that it was time to move forward on other issues. In particular, she expressed some discomfort with the forthrightness expressed by the Supporting Survivors group and their unwillingness to forgive, because forgiveness was central to her understanding of faithful Catholicism.

[T]here is a group in Voice and you probably know who they are in our group, who are angry and who want to sustain that anger. And this, of course, is very hard to reconcile with being a faithful Catholic because you know, the whole thing about forgiveness. If we are faithful Catholics we believe in (a) redemption and (b) forgiveness. And if you are constantly angry and it's directed at people, then you are not giving them the possibility of redemption and you are not forgiving. And, you know, it makes a lot of us very uncomfortable.

By contrast, Grace felt comfortable challenging the Church by supporting the priests who were never suspected of abuse, whom she believed were victims of the sex abuse cover-up, if not the abuse itself. She, like many within the group, was also uneasy with the tenor and intensity of the Supporting Survivors working group: "The Supporting Priests [group] one is the least guilty of [being strident]. It's the least controversial. Definitely the Survivor group and the Structural Change groups [are] the more strident voices. I mean, there's not much to get strident about. 'Hi, Father, oh, isn't that nice.'"

Conflicting Voices

The differences among these three working groups—in terms of their goals, practices, and discourses—became more pronounced as the shock of the scandal receded. Those who supported survivors did not see the need to direct their energies toward priests. Although they did not denounce all priests as guilty of sexual abuse, they believed that their work with survivors would be undermined by speaking out on behalf of the clergy. They were also reluctant to forgo the condemnation that forgiveness and conciliation would entail. The Supporting Survivors group was also wary of refocusing VOTF efforts on structural changes that might displace attention from the origins of the crisis and the continuing needs of its victims. By contrast, VOTFers who worked with the priests believed that a continual focus on the survivors would similarly undermine their efforts in securing the trust of the clergy.

These groups had started in an ad hoc manner, taking the three planks as useful templates to anchor their initial response to the unfolding crisis. However, as time passed, members' identities were increasingly lodged in their activities within these working groups. As the differences within the St. Erasmus chapter intensified, the internal groups increasingly derived their sense of identity and purpose in contrast to the other working groups. A significant amount of this internal tension revolved around the different temporal orientations of the three groups.

The Supporting Survivors group saw the work of VOTF as anchored in the past, in the abuse suffered by the victims. Since the injury could never be undone, the group's work supporting these victims would likewise never end. Theirs was a goal that could never be realized once and for all. There was no future that they could imagine where the injury was surmounted or the support they offered was sufficient. Their support of survivors—in the form of money, empathy, political alliance—constituted an ongoing commitment to be there for the survivors in the present.

By contrast, the Structural Change group's temporal focus was more on reform, and thus future-oriented. Despite their realization that changing the Church might indeed take a "lifetime," and despite disagreement about what changes to pursue, this group could at least hypothetically envision a time when structural changes might be achieved: laity included in governance, women ordained, celibacy elective, and so forth. The future orientation of this group helps to explain the frustration they sometimes expressed about the Supporting Survivors group being stuck in the past and the need to "move on" from the scandal. Although he would not have embraced the project of structural change, Father Francis expressed a similar frustration with the "support the survivor" goal.

The Supporting Priests group conceived of the injustices suffered by priests of integrity as something that could be achieved in the near future, or even in the present. For those priests who faced unresolved accusations of sexual abuse, the Church could act expeditiously, offering judgment and some sort of closure. For priests of integrity—those who were not suspected of any wrongdoing—the group could offer ongoing support. This support was embedded in an iterative present in which members ritualistically reaffirmed their recognition and appreciation of these priests. The periodic commitment to priests of integrity—at the appreciation picnic, at the invited talks and panels, and through annual contributions to the parish—mimicked the Church calendar and, like much ritual, resolved the conflicts and injuries of the past. Compared to the other two working groups, their temporal orientation in an ongoing present meant that the Supporting Priests group experienced a greater sense of success and achievement. They received continual affirmation for their work, particularly from Father Francis, who repeatedly referred to the group as the "conscience of the Church," and from invited priests who called what they did "life-affirming." Their success might reflect the modesty of their ambitions. As Grace admitted, theirs had the least controversial and least risky agenda, one that would be less likely to alienate other parishioners or clergy. Still, it could and did, in its timidity, generate some tension within the larger chapter and among the working groups.

When we began our fieldwork with St. Erasmus VOTF in 2007, the tensions among the three working groups were at their height. The salience of the working groups was apparent in the chapter's weekly agenda. Whereas in 2006 there were only two meetings devoted to working groups, in 2007 approximately one meeting a month involved splitting up into working groups. The tensions were not, however, apparent in the interactions at the other Monday-night meetings. The participants were always polite and cordial. The "etiquette" of the group tacitly discouraged the expression of anger, censure, or even heated disagreement. It was not until we began conducting individual interviews and otherwise informally interacting with members that we became aware of the increasingly sinewy lines of demarcation.

The etiquette of St. Erasmus VOTF more or less resembled the institutional rules that had always governed the laity: one did not openly discuss matters of contention or challenge others' views. According to Jerome P. Baggett the fact that the Church is such a hierarchal organization has taken a "civic toll" on spirited public discussion of political or ethical issues (2008, 182).[5] Of course, members of St. Erasmus VOTF would appear to be exceptional among Catholics in this regard. Yet habits and expectations of a lifetime are remarkably hard to shed. Phil commented on this in regard to the simmering issues within the group: "The Catholic Church for so long has had this attitude that you can't talk. There are huge things we're not supposed to talk about. In a culture where talk is forbidden, talk can become very dangerous."

In my Irish Catholic upbringing, I was never taught appropriate ways to feel and express my anger. When I sit with the reality of the impotency of the laity in relation to Church structures in everything from liturgy, canon law, decision-making, choosing leadership, I realize I have learned my lessons well and I am surprised I have ever found my "voice."

Not surprisingly, given the lifetime of such "lessons," the differences regarding what direction the group should be moving in and how it should conduct itself in pursuing its goals remained veiled, subterranean, or only expressed in what Nina Eliasoph called the "back stage." However, frank discussions did happen on occasion in the monthly steering committee meetings that the group conducted for several years. These meetings were open to all (though this wasn't entirely apparent to every member of the chapter) but were generally attended by the most regular and active members. The steering committee meetings could serve as a backstage, where differences were broached. As the imagined ties found in the origin stories became more attenuated, tensions surfaced periodically. Shirley recalled, for example, that in one of these meetings there was a blunt exchange about the advisability of asking a specific priest to talk to the group that represented tension between the Supporting Survivors and Structural Change groups.[6]

The conflicts were also given voice, albeit indirectly, in general discussions regarding the national VOTF. The cleavages at the national level reflected what was occurring within the St. Erasmus chapter. The parallels allowed the St. Erasmus chapter to engage in the debates but at a remove that did not exact the civic toll that routinely constrained them. Discussing the contentious issues that were roiling the national organization was a way then of relaxing the etiquette that discouraged making disagreement and conflict visible within St. Erasmus VOTF. The national organization thus provided an "other," or a perspective from which St. Erasmus VOTF could articulate and reflect on how to process the emerging conflicts within their group.

In June 2007, for instance, the national VOTF went "public" with the issue of mandatory celibacy by requesting that the Vatican conduct an ecclesiastical review. The request signaled a shift in national strategy. Prior to that time, the national organization, much like St. Erasmus, avoided or downplayed the more controversial issues associated with structural change as a way of bolstering their "mainstream" status within the church. By 2007, the organization was experiencing declining membership and dwindling coffers. Many of the original founders of the organization expressed some skepticism about the shift to a more ambitious agenda for structural change. Jim Post, the first president of VOTF, said, "We've repeatedly rejected that argument, saying that those are not our issues. Even I wonder whether we shouldn't just declare victory and say a lot's been done in five years, the Church is doing better than it was, and then let the other organizations—Call to Action, Future Church, and others that really want to deal with these issues—have the field."[7]

Soon after the national VOTF published its request of the Vatican, the St. Erasmus chapter devoted a Monday-night meeting to talk about the issue. The discussion began by considering the substantive issue of mandatory celibacy and whether it was an appropriate or timely change to pursue. As we have noted, there was not a great deal of consensus on this matter, with many present expressing support for the change personally but greater caution about making it an official part of VOTF's mission. Quickly, however, the discussion shifted from the specific issue of celibacy to the process through which the request for ecclesiastic review emerged out of the national organization. A number of people, even as they endorsed the review itself, questioned the top-down manner in which the change in strategy occurred. They felt as if the process recapitulated the hierarchical structure of the Church and the exclusion of lay voices from the collective conversation.

At this meeting a subtle but significant change occurred in how the differences within the group were experienced and narrated. In criticizing the national organization's unilateral decision to pursue the issue of mandatory celibacy, St. Erasmus VOTF began to see, and talk about, the price of unity and consensus and, more important, the processes through which it is achieved. At the 2008 meeting that Dan Bartley, the newly elected president of the national VOTF, attended, this new skepticism was apparent in their questioning of the more hierarchal, centralized, and professionalized mission he outlined. At this point, the members of St. Erasmus began to adopt an etiquette for expressing, if not resolving, difference. The proximate push to do so, however, was a shake-up in the group itself that led members to unite around their differences.

Peter Leaves: Developing a Successor Story

From the start, Peter connected the group. Thomas much later reflected that Peter "led from the middle" and in doing so "assisted the group in finding its own way." However, that was soon to change. In the fall of 2007, after quietly organizing and directing the weekly meetings for five years, Peter announced at a steering committee meeting that he was moving out of state and would no longer be able to participate in St. Erasmus VOTF. In making the announcement, Peter appeared hesitant and reluctant to make a clean break from the group, but he was emphatic that he had already made up his mind. A few members suggested that he could stay with them on Monday nights. He declined their offers, noting the length and logistics of his commute. And despite their best efforts to persuade him to continue, it became increasingly clear to everyone in the room that Peter was leaving.

Peter insisted that if the group was to survive, they must continue to meet weekly. He was emphatic that were they to switch to monthly meetings, they would end up like other affiliates with declining membership. Expressing his ambivalence about leaving, he admitted that this situation was "a disaster" from an organizational point of view.

The other members of the steering committee concurred that this was a turning point.[8] The extraordinary extent of Peter's contribution to the group also became clear as he distributed a "job description." This was a single-spaced page of tasks including booking and scheduling events, setting up the room, introducing speakers and running the meeting, sending announcements to the press, and sending regular weekly emails. He paid for the webpage/email account and the phone. He managed the arrangements with the parish (mentioning the difficult people and having to finesse them). The list was very long, the work constant and much of it tedious.

While everyone recognized the seriousness of the situation, there was disagreement as to how they should react. It was undeniably a turning point, but the direction in which they would turn was not foregone. Some who were present that night, even while saddened by Peter's leaving, were optimistic that the group could make the transition effectively. Victoria, who up to this point had been a regular, but not central, figure in the group, later recounted her reaction.

I could see that everybody was saying, "We can't go on without Peter." A lot of people were saying it. And I kept saying, "Nonsense," you know? I thought it was a very vulnerable moment partly because there was this mindset that we *couldn't* manage without Peter. And I knew that we *could* manage without Peter. And so, you know, I helped push along. We got the list of what he did and we got people to volunteer.

Others within the group agreed that meting out the regular tasks could be done with little disruption. But Phil asked that they slow down, describing Peter's leaving as a loss, a sort of death. "We need time to mourn and grieve," he said. "Let's not move too fast." Eventually it was decided that they needed to regroup soon. A special meeting of the group, open to anyone, was scheduled for the following week to begin an hour before the regular public meetings.

By the following month's steering committee meeting, Peter was gone. Although everyone was anxious about the effect of his absence on the group, they saw this crisis of leadership as an opportunity for the group to reconsider the direction it had been moving in. In particular, the committee discussed the three goals and the corresponding working groups. Shirley observed that there was not a lot of communication or exchange among the groups, reflecting the etiquette of civic silencing we mentioned earlier. She went on to say that after initially dividing up into different groups, people tended to stay put. Grace noted that the focus of the three groups had changed and they needed to take time to reconsider the changes. She believed that while in the beginning the survivors were the rightful focus, the group's goals had broadened.

Toward the end of 2007, the chapter began to shift away from the regular working groups and toward an agenda that was more educational.

There were more speakers, films, and readings on topics ranging from Church history to theology. Not everyone agreed that abandoning the working groups was a good idea. In particular, Shirley raised the issue of whether the meetings were serving the goals of the group. She commented, "We are not just a social club. We need to remind ourselves of why we are doing this." Recognizing the legitimacy of Shirley's concern, Grace mentioned that someone had recently asked her why they did all this "education," referring to the speakers, readings, films, and discussions of Catholic history and theology. She admitted that it took hours for her to come up with an answer to the question. "This group is about lay empowerment. We will be running things. We need to be educated."

Sarah made a similar observation about the necessity of the laity taking up responsibility for maintaining the Church in the future. For her the group's efforts to educate themselves was much more than a self-improvement project: it would ensure the future of the Catholic Church.

With all of the education that we have received, the readings, the lectures, I realize more clearly that the practice as we know it is going to be a lot more difficult. The Church is compressing. There aren't going to be enough priests to do things the way we are used to do it. I don't know how long I'll live but there may come a time when it's going to be hard to find Mass conveniently.

Her response expressed a dramatic shift in how the chapter envisioned its mission. They now understood that "changing the Church" meant changing themselves. The meeting ended with a general consensus that St. Erasmus VOTF was entering a new chapter in the life of the affiliate. In light of this realization, there was a noticeable change in the way the group talked about the different planks. Whereas they had been a source of dissensus, albeit suppressed under an etiquette of civic silence, there was now a clear recognition of the benefits of difference.

I see the groups as being intermingled—that each one needs the other. So, I mean, Structural Change needs the experience of the victims to help us to organize what we need to do, and they need structural change. And we all need the support of the priests' group. Because we have so many priests who have been hurt by this. And who have put a lot on the line. You know, they're the ones that are going to be breaking through to their brother priests to come to realize that you've got to come down and sit at the table and figure out what's going on. (Shirley)

With this change, the group's constitution and its persistence began to eclipse the increasingly separate and sometimes competing goals of structural change, supporting survivors, and supporting priests of integrity. The mutual and enduring ties and obligations that they had forged over the years emerged to define the group and its mission. Commenting on the crisis of a declining number of priests and what that might portend for the future of the Catholic Church, Sarah stated simply, "What are we going to hang on to? We have to hang on. If you don't have a priest and you don't have Communion, you have to hang on to each other more."

Rather than simply reflecting on the changes they had achieved in the Church, members of St. Erasmus VOTF began to recognize how they had changed through their interactions with one another. For Phil, Margaret, Thomas, and others in the group, collective identity and collective purpose had merged at the point where the "we-ness" of the group became the "why" of the group. As Phil went on to comment, "And as Sister Bridget was always fond of saying, 'We all have a little piece of the truth.' She says it isn't all wrapped up in the cardinal or the bishop or the priest. Every individual has a little piece of the truth and together we should be finding it with each other."

As promised, Peter's break from the group was clean. All of the work that he had been tirelessly and quietly doing for the first few years had been almost seamlessly transferred to various members of the group. And almost one year later, they were still there meeting every Monday night, raising money for survivors, offering an ongoing series of speakers, films, and discussions, and (at least for some of them) periodically engaging in more public acts of protest. Reflecting on the transition, some of the regular members seemed pleased but somewhat surprised by their success. Ralph expressed this new sense of collective agency.

Well, it seemed to me, you know, in the beginning, and for quite some time, Peter was really the impetus behind the whole group. I thought, and I was wondering, if the group was going to fail [when he left]. But it didn't. I mean, there were enough people that took right over. Usually ruling by committee doesn't work. But in this case it seemed to. Well, I think it's gotten stronger.

Peter returned one or two times in the following years, but never as a regular member of the group. Yet he remained a presence even in his absence. His leaving wasn't just a turning point, it was a turning point that the group acknowledged and continued to weave into its story of itself. The organizational crisis of his leaving became part of the culture of the group. The story of his leaving affirmed them as a group even as it venerated Peter. There was near consensus that he was responsible for giving them a sense of direction, as well as pride in their capacity to continue along that path once he was gone.

It would be easy to characterize Peter's role in St. Erasmus VOTF as a case of "great man" leadership: the group succeeded and persisted because of his individual talents. He certainly was a "great man" to his fellow VOTFers at St. Erasmus. And while we would not dispute his talent, unwavering commitment, and many contributions to the group, there is another way to understand the story of Peter and, perhaps just as important, how that story was told by the group. Notably, he did not figure into their narratives as a charismatic leader. The words that were most frequently used to describe him were quiet, reserved, humble, and even "uncomfortable." Significantly, the extent of the work he performed was only fully revealed at the moment he stopped doing it.

As we mentioned earlier, Peter's leadership style was more pastoral than charismatic. He seemed almost to enact the role of parish priest. He would call the meeting to order, begin with a prayer, and introduce the speaker or program—and it was Peter who insisted on weekly attendance. He was respected and earned the deference typically given to a beloved priest. We were, in fact, certain after his announcement that he was leaving that our nascent project studying this chapter of VOTF would come to a premature end, that if anything this would be a study of movement decline. That did not happen. His departure offered the group an opportunity to step out of their role as parishioners, to become, as Thomas put it, "agents." Peter's leaving "activated" the group such that the cultural values of dialogue, pastoral power, voice, and religious agency were "put to work" more broadly. His exit required that they become responsible, deliberate, and self-directing as a group—"adult baptized Catholics," to use their phrasing—in a way that they hadn't been. It turned out that Peter's last and perhaps greatest act of leadership had been to leave and, in leaving, show the others that they could carry on.

Peter's leaving disrupted the group's origin story. As Owens (2008) observes, origin stories can only bend so far before they break. Challengers successfully negotiate turning points by producing a successor story that prevents such breakage. Successor stories can offer a means of negotiating the knitting of multiplicity within the group that was first imagined in the origin story. In addition, revisiting earlier topics, they provide for the continued integrity of their origin by maintaining a link with the past. Successor stories manage and reconfigure the temporal continuity that we have argued is essential for a group's reflexivity. Groups are continually responding to the questions "Who are we now?" and "What do we do next?" At turning points, successor stories offer narrative sense making.

Peter's abrupt leaving tore at the fabric of the origin story and changed the St. Erasmus VOTFers' course of action. Peter's pastoral guidance had allowed disparate interests a voice, harmonized the distinct projects of the working groups, and mended relations between members. As Juliana reflected, "I think that some of the survivor people felt maybe we were spending too much time on other things, and really this was the most important. And nobody wanted to say it wasn't. But I do think that, going back to Peter, he had a way of settling the waters." Now he was gone and members had to change course to face issues of multiplicity. In the face of submerged conflicts, they also needed a new narrative for how they would continue without his leadership. They needed a new scripting of how they would persist beyond his departure.

Approximately twenty people showed up at the pre-meeting the following week. They quickly decided to adopt a team approach to leading the group and running the weekly meetings. Someone suggested that they assign jobs for a three-month period, at which time they would rotate. Soon, however, the group rejected this process as being too cumbersome. Finally, the work that Peter had primarily undertaken during the past five years was parceled out item by item to the ten people willing to work on a regular basis.

Through this process a successor story developed. In this narrative Peter's departure prompted the group to collectively exercise a kind of pastoral self-care that accommodated multiplicity. As Juliana recalled of that period, "So differences in the group, they all came together, really." In this emergent narrative, multiplicity becomes the basis for agency.

In the story this newfound sense of collective agency prompted greater individual effort and cooperation in taking on Peter's former responsibilities. As Sarah noted, "I wanted it to keep going. And for my own self, I knew I had to step up a little more." This was a sentiment expressed by a number of others who assumed Peter's former tasks. In the narrative Sarah and others also pointed to another motivation—to continue Peter's legacy: "But I honestly wonder if we just didn't—We just owed it to him that we wouldn't let it fall apart." St. Erasmus VOTFers recognized that, in their multiplicity, each member could make a distinct contribution to a project that Peter had helped them build.

Conclusion: Cohesion out of Conflict

Conflict and difference can strengthen group cohesion when it is organized in such a way as to operate as "a vehicle or culture carrier that transports meta-meanings fashioned from the assemblages of logistical decisions" (Ghaziani 2008, 304). In the case of St. Erasmus VOTF, the factions that emerged around the three planks threatened at one point to divide, and perhaps even dissolve, the group. By 2008, these differences were transformed into a narrative of group identity that transcended any particular goal. This transformation was achieved in part through the group's ability to develop a discourse for talking about and reflecting on the role of difference. Seeing the conflicts and direction of the national organization offered a stark contrast to their own sense of purpose. It also offered a "safe" way of articulating conflict, and a rationale for embracing it. Rather than the singular and top-down directives from the national organization, St. Erasmus VOTF began to develop a new set of "meta-meanings" about who they were as a group.

The concerns of some of the Supporting Priests group, for instance, converged at points with the goals of the Structural Change group. For at least some Supporting Priests VOTFers, mandatory celibacy (as opposed to elective celibacy) was seen as a major culprit in sustaining the solitary life of a parish priest. And, in their concern for the needs and rights of priests, the group recognized the relative lack of power that diocesan priests had in the Church. It was the Vatican and the Curia that exercised the greatest power and that thus deserved the strongest censure. Like the Supporting Survivors group, the Supporting Priests group favored a form of pastoral justice, but for them it was more for priests whom they understood to be unrecognized victims of the scandal.

In short, they began to discern those matters of "higher order consensus" that defined the group. Woven through all of the working groups was a commitment to pastoral care and an agreement that the Church's principles of faith (as opposed to "culture" or man-made rules) were not to be challenged. There was broad agreement that the Curia and hierarchy were shrouded in secrecy and privilege and substantial agreement that parish priests were, like the laity themselves, relatively powerless within that hierarchy. Finally, and perhaps most importantly, they reaffirmed that they had a strong commitment to open dialogue and collaboration and the differences they often excavate. Referring to others within St. Erasmus VOTF, Thomas conceded,

I think what those people do is significant. . . . Two years ago I might have given them a long list of instructions. I don't have anything to say to them now. I believe that these people have wrestled with their conscience and they are somewhere. And where they are is important. . . . What they say by their appearance is important. I will support that whatever way I can, even though there may be things that they want to do that I'm not going to do. I'm disappointed because they're not down here on the sidewalk. But on the other hand, they're the only ones doing anything. And the St. Erasmus people in particular, you know, I just find it—We must be doing something. Right? And I finally decided I think I know what it is. We shine light on the truth. And not well, and we don't know how to respond to it, you know? The appropriate and adequate response doesn't exist yet. And we come together as a group of people. Probably no two of whom agree on what it is we need to do. But they come every Monday.

The second contingent event that solidified these cultural shifts, making them "resinous," or sticky, was Peter leaving. The organizational "disaster" of Peter's departure presented an opportunity to enact this metanarrative. His exit led to what Ghaziani calls "assemblages of logistical decision," or concrete tasks through which members could build a culture of diversity. Being attached to key recurring decisions—such as scheduling weekly meetings, managing finances, facilitating discussion, issuing press releases, and so forth—created a "resinous culture framework" that gave their valuing of difference a traction in the ongoing life of the group.

Seventeen years on, the working groups are now a historical artifact, and the group no longer meets every Monday throughout the year. Still pursuing its project to "Keep the Faith, Change the Church," the St. Erasmus chapter is reflexively evaluating their long arc of activism and their future. Some key members have raised the prospect of coordination with another chapter as a way forward. Thomas is one who broached this idea, but he wasn't sure that the two groups would readily knit together. The St. Erasmus chapter, he observed, was built on a multiplicity of voices and the ability to nurture community in this diversity. This is their story, until another successor emerges.

FIVE

Conclusion

Throughout this book we have described and analyzed the stories, both collective and individual, that St. Erasmus VOTF told about their experiences challenging the Church. Through their origin stories they articulated a compulsion to act that was triggered by the ontological threat to their sense of what it means to be a faithful Catholic. Through their successor stories they recovered their sense of agency and reconstituted themselves as different, but no less faithful, Catholics. It is now time for us to provide narrative closure to the story that we, as sociologists, are telling about St. Erasmus. Stories, then, about stories. We have already gestured to our story when we wrote in the introduction that our account of St. Erasmus VOTF is "an all-too-familiar story of identities under stress, about institutional betrayal and the renegotiation of trust, about commitment and the meaning of justice." What, then have we learned about collective identity, trust, and justice in the context of social movements?

Collective Identity

At the eleventh anniversary meeting of St. Erasmus VOTF, the twenty members who were present reflected on what they had accomplished over the years. Everyone present believed that there was still much to do, but also felt that they had made real progress. They also considered the future of the group. Fewer people were attending the weekly meetings. Those who continued to be active were getting older. Indeed, some of the core members had recently died or become gravely ill. St. Erasmus VOTF had not been successful in attracting new or younger members. As the shock of the scandal waned, even as its global scope became tragically apparent, it was more difficult to attract others to the cause. There was some discussion of futility and how to maintain their resolve in the face of standing up to a "Goliath."

Thomas interrupted the dispiriting talk of past accomplishments and future directions by suggesting that the most important question they needed to ask themselves was not what to do next, but "who are we?" He said, "Lots of Catholics read that *Globe* article eleven years ago and knew about the scandal, but the vast majority did nothing." By contrast, "We all reacted the way we did at the time because of who we were." He went on to say that posing and answering the question of "who are we" eleven years later "will point us in the right direction."

Taking up the question of identity, one member said that the difference between VOTF and others who did nothing was that they were "awakened." The term hinted that the scandal activated something in them that was present but dormant. As to the issue of futility, they agreed that their continued presence was in and of itself an accomplishment. And maybe their small numbers did not diminish their mission. Maureen likened VOTF to rescuers during the Holocaust, noting that most people were not rescuers, they were a tiny minority—but important nonetheless.

In asserting the primacy of the question "who are we," Thomas revealed himself to be an acute observer of social movements and collective action. There is broad agreement among social movement researchers that collective identity is a critical basis for collective action. Some take a stronger position, claiming that it is more than a foundation that facilitates effective action; it is a predicate for action. This latter position insists that collective identity is necessary for any type of collective action to occur (Holland et al. 1998). In this book, we make an even stronger claim regarding collective identity: that it is not merely a facilitator or even a predicate of action; it can itself be a type of collective challenge to the hegemonic narrative of order and hierarchy. Reconstituting ourselves, making up a group where none had existed, is, or can be, a formidable challenge to those in power, particularly for challengers within. How were these inexperienced and initially conflicted challengers able to create and sustain a collective identity? And what might their struggle to construct a collective identity teach us about the processes through which identity is forged?

First, the case of St. Erasmus VOTF powerfully illustrates the emergent nature of collective identity. Collective identity is not an entity that is constructed once and for all; it is, as Baumann claims, a verb and not a noun. As such, it is active, changing, unstable, and emergent. It is work and trouble. Groups do not have an identity; they are in the process of continually constructing one. Yet despite its processual and emergent character, it is undeniable that identity is experienced as having a form, a shape, or a thingness to it. Indeed, the powerful claim of identity on ourselves and others—on pointing us in the right direction, for instance—may lie precisely in our sense of it not as emerging out of the flow of time and experience but rather as something solid and abiding, existing on a different plane: prior to, above, and beyond the exigencies of life or fate. For example, I may know that I have changed, but my sense is that there is some underlying "I" that has undergone these changes. The same could be said for groups. Therein lies the contradiction at the heart of identity.[1] But if identity is a process and all that that entails—changing, fragile, and contingent—how does it come to feel like a more or less stable, resilient, and abiding aspect of who we are?

We propose that the phenomenological experience of identity as entity—as opposed to process—is a reflection of the multidimensional and axial nature of collective identity. By axial we mean that collective identity needs to be envisioned in relation to the sameness–difference polarities of each dimension, rather than focusing on one end. In other words, the sense of a "we" is a contingent result of a tensile stability achieved along three axes of variation. Reflecting on this insight, Ghaziani notes that while all groups "must contend with the logics of sameness and difference" (2008, 117), existing theoretical accounts of collective identity tend to slight the "sameness" end of the continuum in terms of the external relational axis. At the same time, these accounts tend to neglect the role of "difference" in terms of intragroup relations. We propose a corrective to this tendency by attending to the ways groupness emerges out of the internal contradictions entailed in being both "same as" and "different from."

For instance, in regard to the temporal dimension of identity, a challenging group perceives itself as different from, but also continuous with, its past and future. Recognizing both continuity (sameness) and change (difference), the group can narrate a story about itself. It can, in a sense, emplot itself. Similarly, even though groups construct boundaries that delineate themselves from outsiders, thus inflecting difference, they also routinely transcend those boundaries in recognizing similarities with those outside of the group. Their sense of "who we are" thus emerges from perceived similarities ("We are like rescuers during the Holocaust," "We are like faithful Catholics") as much as from differences ("We are not like those who did nothing") with selected others. Finally, the internal solidarity of the group relies on all sorts of commonalities among members, but it also finds expression in the group's capacity to contain difference and even conflict.

At various junctures in St. Erasmus VOTF's history—beginning with their own sense of not being "rabble-rousers" or dissidents and ending with their discovery of faith in those very roles—they narrated themselves into being and doing. Along the way, they faced significant challenges as they navigated the temporal and relational axes of identity. In their case, the initial identity crisis occurred along the axis of temporality. In order to act, they needed to reconcile their longstanding identity as obedient and deferential Catholics with the urge to stand up to the Church hierarchy. The second crisis entailed redefining and reestablishing their relationships with those outside of the group, defining themselves as both "a part of" and "apart from" the Church. Finally, they ran into trouble when dissension within the group emerged around goals and how they should be pursued. At this point, the group needed to become capacious enough to hold differences among members.

At each of these junctures, or turning points, the development and maintenance of a collective identity necessitated reestablishing the tension—rather than resolving it—between sameness and difference. The challenge, in fact, was to avoid sliding entirely toward one end of the axis. For instance, the rupture they experienced when the scandal broke—the sense of falling off a cliff—became an origin story that enabled agency by narratively denying it. But that rupture—that sense of being suspended between before and after—could not sustain agency over time. The evocative metaphor of "falling" suggests that there is no traction, and thus no "movement," social or otherwise. In order to achieve the capacity to act collectively, they had to retrieve a past that contained the seeds of their challenge, thus grounding their actions and establishing the temporal continuity we associate with identity. Who they were, both individually and collectively, and what they were experiencing was undeniably different from their prior life within the Church, but they were not entirely discontinuous from that life either. With time, as the scandal, and thus their origin, receded, St. Erasmus VOTF began to narrate their continued transformation from naive to knowing. They thus constructed a life story by tacking back and forth between the "sameness" with their past and their newly discovered "difference" from it.

St. Erasmus VOTF experienced the second "crisis" when they encountered the negative judgments of others who were denying the group's claim to being true Catholics. Whereas most fledgling challenging groups initially face the opposite challenge—how to demarcate a boundary that defines them as distinctive and establish a clear "us" and "them"— St. Erasmus VOTF struggled to locate themselves within the larger Church. Because they did not want to separate themselves entirely from the mainstream laity, or to stand in complete opposition to the hierarchy, they needed to establish themselves as an embedded group with porous boundaries. Ironically, receiving affirmation from those outsiders that their group was in fact composed of exemplary lay Catholics— rather than dissidents or troublemakers—eventually sharpened their sense of being different from other Catholics. Once their status as Catholics in good standing was recognized, the group felt confident enough to begin to reflect on how they were distinctive in their faith and service. This sense in turn emboldened them to be more ambitious in their pursuit of change. There was no trace of the reluctance and ambivalence they experienced when they first joined VOTF. When in 2008, Edwina Gately, an invited speaker from the national VOTF, exhorted them to "be haughty—Jesus was," the room nodded in total agreement.

Whether as a result of pivoting internally, or simply because after five years they had, as Alfred Schutz puts it, "grown old together," differences and conflict within the group became apparent. The identity work that the group needed to do if it was to persist was to find a way to contain those differences by finding common ground. Failing to balance sameness and difference among the members would have led to one of two outcomes: the group would have devolved into destructive dissensus or narrowed to a singularity. Either outcome would have prevented the development of a metanarrative about "who we are" rather than "what are we to do?" It was the prospect of singularity, however, that initially threatened the group's cohesion. When the differences among members regarding strategies and goals first appeared, they were not expressed openly. The conflicts were masked by a spurious consensus. Maintaining the civil politeness not only suppressed the conflict (its ostensible goal), it also prevented productive conversations about what united them in the face of infighting. When the group eventually realized that one of their foundational goals, their raison d'être, was voice, something they had been long denied within the Church and even within the national VOTF organization, they embraced their differences—or the group's capacity to work with those differences—as a central and defining part of their identity.

While we have focused on challengers within, we believe that all challenging groups—and indeed all groups—construct a collective identity along these axes. Whether we are talking about families, corporations, civic groups, or activist groups, the construction of a group identity and thus the capacity to act is predicated on sustaining a position of sameness and difference. Family stories are told and retold in part to link the present to the past, but they are also told to reassure one another that the family has transcended that past.

Movement stories must be resilient enough to maintain the torque between sameness and difference (temporally and relationally) as circumstances change. Failure to do so, getting "stuck" at one pole, is often an important reason for movement decline. Lynn Owens's (2008) study of the decline of the Amsterdam squatters movement illustrates how the movement's origin story, which initially provided a thread that bound diverse challengers in a series of contentious actions with local authorities over control of city spaces, ultimately hardened and prevented the evolution of the movement. According to Owens's account, at various points the group failed to realize the productive tensions along each of the three axes.

Small groups had squatted in neglected areas of Amsterdam for a good portion of the 1970s even though their actions were decentralized, pragmatic, and not tied together with a narrative skein that offered a comprehensive political vision. This all changed in February 1980. A violent and protracted battle between squatters and police (in which army tanks were eventually used to overcome the protesters) over the occupation of a building on Vondelstraat birthed an origin story. The narrative was of a radical movement bent on transforming power over urban place and space. The origin story provided the footing for diverse activists to join together against the injustice of established power. However, after experiencing a series of setback with authorities as well as increasing dissension among their ranks, the squatters did not reformulate their origin story, nor were they able to produce successor stories that gave them a way of moving forward. Retelling what was apparently the same story, they failed to incorporate narratives of temporality or of change. Second, the squatters were never able to develop a metadiscourse on the internal–relational axis in order to achieve some sort of unity out of multiplicity. There were no stories concerning the division of labor or of divergent but meaningful contributions to their ongoing challenge. Finally, with regard to the self–other axis, their collective identity stifled the capacity of the group to acknowledge or imagine success vis-à-vis the city government short of an almost revolutionary transformation. Thus, for example, the city's offer to the squatters to take control of a series of squats to provide subsidized housing for poor families with children was viewed as an unacceptable compromise. The collective identity of the movement ossified around a narrow radicalism that increasingly prevented a sense of having any mutual interests with their opponents or other groups.

The defection of radical white feminists from the New Left in the 1970s offers another case of an internal collective identity crisis that was not successfully resolved. According to Benita Roth (2004), the white feminists within the New Left experienced mounting dissatisfaction with the second-class status they were given within the movement. Relegated to "housekeeping" roles and exploited sexually, the women began to consider establishing an autonomous movement. From their point of view, this would require abandoning their identity within the New Left and establishing a new radical feminist collective identity. Since most of the radical feminists had acquired their political experience within the New Left, their preexisting commitment created a dilemma for them even in the face of their mounting disaffection. They resolved this dilemma by claiming that they were no more similar to the men in the New Left than they were to mainstream (chauvinist) American men when it came to women's struggle. Radical males were thus redefined as just "men" (Densmore 1971). Whereas before their defection white radical feminists "saw a boundary between themselves and other women, and even other feminists," they now recognized that all women in a sexist society were "alike."

From the vantage point of the New Left, the defection of feminists clearly signaled a failure of the movement to manage internal multiplicity. "New Left organizations such as the SDS [Students for a Democratic Society] could have tried to co-opt emerging feminists by adopting their agenda outright; they could have coexisted with new feminist groups by forming or encouraging women's caucuses within existing radical organizations. . . . But the pervasive response by male leftists was not one of co-optation or cooperation; it was denigration" (Roth 2004, 63).

Roth, citing Echols (1989), writes that the failure of the New Left to accommodate feminists within the movement was a result of the enshrinement of race and class as privileged categories of oppression. Thus the men within the New Left may "have reacted badly to activists who were more or less like them and claiming a label of oppression" (63). Usually we think of infighting and fracture as resulting from perceptions of difference among members, but in this case it was the perceived similarity (in terms of their privilege) that led to the response of men and, according to some, the eventual demise of the New Left (Gitlin 1987).

In short, by insisting that women were "more or less the same as them," the movement slid toward that end of the internal relational axis.

Whereas the New Left failed, in part, because of the defection of feminists within the group, other groups fail because of the absence of infighting, or at least a deficit of diversity of thought and experience. In *Social Movements, Political Violence, and the State* (1995), Donatella della Porta examines the processes through which Italian and German activists in the 1960s and 1970s became radicalized to the point that they were willing to employ violence. A crucial part of this process is the construction of a particular type of collective identity based on a near total isolation from social networks outside of the group, an intensification of social relationships and ideological intolerance within the group, and biographic rupture in which members were "resocialized" in such a way as to unmoor them from their pasts.

In terms of our axial model of collective identity, della Porta's description of the processes of radicalization represents a slide along the external relational axis toward total difference—indeed, near isolation—from the nonradicalized world: "Thus, in time, the number and the extent of channels of communication between 'inside' and 'outside' are dramatically reduced" (161). There was also a corresponding shift toward the "sameness" pole of the internal relational axis whereby "dense social networks of comrade-friends proliferated and alternative value systems emerged" (161). This worldview was sustained by the terrorist organizations demanding of their members "complete renunciation of all the external ties that could endanger the group; the sharing of all possessions, each member becoming nothing else than a small part of the whole; and the mortification of private needs and the abnegation of the self for the organizational needs" (179). Individuals' participation in the group and their willingness to use violence was also predicated on a complete temporal rupture with their past. Following Berger and Luckmann (1966), della Porta likens the process of resocialization—in its affective and totalizing nature—to primary socialization. One Italian activist described the rapid and total change in his life: "There is . . . something that I find hard to explain: it is the very high speed at which I precipitated [into the movement]. From [my] first approach, from this curiosity about the new environment, to a more totalistic activism, to my immediately embracing political militancy . . . there were three or four months" (149).

Della Porta describes the cumulative effect of these shifts as "group implosion" (164). The phrase conjures the image of a group collapsing into itself. Rather than the leakage of members experienced by the

New Left, these groups lost the necessary tension between sameness and difference by sliding almost entirely to the "sameness" end internally and the "difference" end externally. The road to implosion was itself an emergent process: della Porta asserts that while these group processes leading to insularity, ideological purity, and extreme homogeneity facilitated the use of violence, subsequent violence tended to "produce a closed and intolerant counterculture" (164).

Clearly, the terrorist organizations della Porta studied developed a collective identity constructed on the extreme ends of the various axes. But did this location lead to the destabilization or demise of the groups, or impede their capacity to act? According to della Porta, it did.

[T]he internal dynamics took over completely once the extremist groups went underground. . . . Of course, clandestinity by definition entails material and psychological isolation. . . . Each successive turn of the spiral reduces the group's strategic options, making it a prisoner of its own version of reality. Under pressures produced by the "implosion" . . . most underground organizations . . . did not survive for long. (98)

These various cases illustrate that not only do all groups develop a collective identity along these axes, they must constantly and inescapably grapple with the logics of sameness and difference.

Rather than a stable, familiar, and bounded sense of "who I am" or "who we are," identity is at best a provisional—and improvisational—reckoning with the contradictions and multiplicity of being, of possibility. Moreover, it takes work to sustain the tautness that makes identity phenomenologically "real." Collective identity is never a settled matter, but it becomes unsettled in fairly predictable ways. At best, it can be conceived of as a stake in the ground that is threatened when circumstances or events push a group toward one endpoint of an axis, creating a type of identity "crisis." And without some sort of reparative identity work, the group's capacity to act is threatened. When this happens, barring some sort of corrective action, groups may implode, as did the terrorist groups della Porta studied. They might also "explode" in the sense that they lose all that is distinctive and defining about themselves. This might occur as a result of excessive assimilation or excessive internal diversity, conflict, or heterogeneity.

Ghaziani (2011) considers this possibility in the case of postgay collective identity construction. He examines what he refers to as the pendulating shifts from difference and sameness in how Princeton University's Pride Alliance, the local LGBT student group, constructs its collective identity.[2] His assumption is that naming is an important part of collective identity construction. Tracing the processes of naming and re-naming over a thirty-eight-year period (1972–2010), Ghaziani observed two trends along what we would call the internal relational axis and the external relational axis.

First, the Pride Alliance had become much more internally diverse since the first gay organization was founded in 1972 for gay men and women. Over the years LGBT student organizing became increasingly complex, necessitating a shift from a "gay plus one" naming strategy (i.e., gay; gay and lesbian; gay, lesbian, bi, trans; etc.) toward a strategy that attempts to define a boundary while not being specific about who is inside (or outside) of it. Ghaziani calls this strategy "intra-group identity muting."

At the same time that the student groups became internally more di-verse, they were becoming more assimilated with mainstream (straight) culture. This trend led to a parallel strategy of intergroup inclusion. "[I]dentity construction in a post-gay era is motivated less by drawing boundaries against the dominant group and more by building bridges toward it (and thus blurring the boundaries). Although collective iden-tity still requires a sense of groupness, it is now less dependent on dif-ferences (Gamson 1997; Seidman 1997) and motivated instead by per-ceived commonalities" (117).

Although Ghaziani does not explicitly discuss the temporal dimen-sion of collective identity, because of the genealogical method he used (tracing the successive names of various student groups over time), it is discernible in his data. As with the internal and external axes, the tem-poral also takes on a "pendulating" character between the poles of same-ness (continuity) and difference (change). Indeed, one officer of the Pride Alliance observed that the name—in its ambiguity and capaciousness—might stand the test of time: "With a name like Pride Alliance, we can be more inclusive and also leave room open to incorporate other groups in the future" (112). In other words, the name itself provides a stable and continuous aspect of the group, even as the group anticipates changes in its membership over time.

As Ghaziani's research suggests, each of these three dimensions, as well as the relations among them, is dialogic and dilemmic. Joshua Gamson captures this character of collective identity, describing it as the "queer dilemma": stable collective boundaries are both the basis for oppression (in the case of marginalized groups) and the basis for political empower-ment. The blurring or muting of boundaries might lessen the oppression but also undermine the potency of political claims. On the other hand, inscribing the marginalized identity, while potentially empowering, may be complicit with those systems of meaning that are the basis for oppression. Notably, Gamson cautions that this dilemma cannot be resolved by adopting either a difference (boundary maintenance) strategy or, alternatively, by abandoning boundaries altogether. "Secure boundaries and stabilized identities," he notes, "are necessary not in general, but in the specific" (1995, 402). The challenge for students of social movements is to clarify what those specifics might be. When, in other words, do groups need to do identity work along one axis rather than another, and in doing so, when do they need to inflect sameness versus difference?

The research on collective identity construction offers a number of "specifics" that might affect the timing and type of identity trouble a group experiences. These would include characteristics of recruits or members to the group, the precipitating events of the movement, challenges to the group boundaries, and cohort effects associated with the formation of a challenging group.

Characteristics of Recruits

In the case of St. Erasmus VOTF a general lack of activist experience, or even a lack of any autobiographical affinity with activism, may have made it more likely that one of the initial challenges the group faced was of temporal discontinuity. The fact that there was no story, either collective or individual, that scripted their activism meant that one needed to be written, retrieved, or retold.

Indeed, two stories needed to be constructed to achieve a degree of continuity after the eruption of the scandal. They each had to narrate a "story of me as a group member" and a "story of my group" (Ashmore, Deaux, and McLaughlin-Volpe 2004). The first story recounts an individual member's past, present, and future. If successful in reestablishing continuity, such a story narrates a meaningful path to their participation. For the members of St. Erasmus VOTF, many told a similar story of standing up to unjust authority within and outside of the Church, which rendered their unlikely challenge meaningful and much less unlikely. Since they were challengers within, the "story of my group" had to reconcile the challenging group (St. Erasmus VOTF) story with the Catholic Church group story. In their case, the reconciliation took the form of retrieving the history of Vatican II. The story of Vatican II served a dual purpose: it provided a warrant for the active challenge of VOTF and it renarrated the Church as the type of institution that would accommodate that challenge.

Roth's study of radical feminists defecting from the New Left, how-ever, demonstrates it is not simply the lack of experience that problem-atizes the temporal dimension of identity. Indeed, Roth observes that "from the standpoint of fashioning a new feminist collective identity, there is much that is problematic in already being committed to an ex-isting group" (2004, 49). In other words, their prior commitment and loyalty to left politics was an impediment to the formation of a splinter group. "Narratives of emerging white women's liberation show the en-ergy that it took for white feminists to actually separate from their par-ent movement" (Roth 2004, 51). In order to proceed, the women had to actively renarrate their past ("story of me as a group member") as well as the New Left ("story of my group") in order to make investments in their autonomous movement.

Of course, not all groups comprise inexperienced membership or mem-bers with conflicted loyalties. According to Kathleen Blee, the members of most of the small fledgling groups she studied had long histories of activism in similar groups and were often simultaneously involved with multiple challenging groups.

Some activists even resisted the idea that their group had a particular starting point at all. For them, grassroots activism is continuous. Groups don't begin; they simply emerge from previous efforts. Likewise, grassroots groups don't die. They are absorbed into a flow of subsequent activism or enter what Verta Taylor describes as periods of "abeyance" to be revived later. (2012, 17)

In light of the salience of origin stories among many activist groups, this view of activism, as temporally seamless and relationally boundaryless, is clearly not universal. What made these groups distinctive is their status as fledging groups. Blee describes them as "without a firm set of collective expectations that define 'who we are' and 'the ways things are'" (2012, 7). Members' involvement in any given group was relatively recent, and at the same time their experience with other activist groups was fairly broad; their processes were experimental and their goals open-ended. In short, it may be these characteristics of participants and the emergent groups that shaped their comparatively weak sense of a collective identity.

Precipitating Events

The events precipitating the formation of a challenging group is a sec-ond factor that shapes the nature and sequence of identity work a group faces. For VOTF, the precipitant was a scandal or, to use Jasper's term, a "moral shock." As we discussed earlier, the phenomenological experience of shock is a sort of temporal suspension or rupture that can be immediately enabling, but in the long run, disabling. In order for the group to persist, some traction needs to be reestablished by constructing a narrative path forward in order to gain a sense of agency.

By contrast, Armstrong and Crage (2013) describe the construction of what they call "the Stonewall myth"—that is, the story that the Stonewall riots were the origin of gay liberation. Armstrong and Crage point out that the police raids at the Stonewall Inn were not unprecedented; rather they were routine matters, both in New York and in other large cities. Nor were the riots at Stonewall unprecedented; similar riots had occurred in the decade before Stonewall. Indeed, it was the longstanding pattern of police oppression that gradually led to the increasingly militant and organized response of gay men and women. This preparation, in turn, enabled gays to exploit the political opportunity presented by Stonewall. As one activist at the time explained, "I immediately knew that this was the spark we had been waiting for years" (2013, 737). This curious statement suggests that there was a preexisting "we" who had been waiting for a politically resonant spark to mobilize and solidify a national movement. As with most origin myths, Stonewall depicted a rupture, a beginning. However, although Stonewall was mythologized as shocking and thus unanticipated, it was not immediately experienced that way. It achieved that mythic standing only retrospectively through commemoration in an annual gay pride parade. Ironically, the commemoration has succeeded by both remembering the events at the Stonewall Inn and forgetting the raids and riots that preceded Stonewall. Whereas St. Erasmus VOTF had to repair a rupture by recuperating a personal and institutional past, gay liberation had to construct a rupture by suppressing a history of similar oppression.[3]

Boundary Challenges

In addition to characteristics of members and movement precipitants, a group's collective identity is a product of events in its environment to which a group must respond. To this point, Lesley Wood observes, "Explicit discussion of identity and identification take place at particular points in movement activity. . . . [I]dentity only becomes an issue when the existing boundaries of that identity are being challenged or defined" (2012, 114). Often these challenges are mounted by outsiders attempting to align the group with negative values or other stigmatized groups. Joshua Gamson describes such an effort to disqualify the International Gay and Lesbian Alliance from receiving United Nations consultative status by focusing on the presence of the North American Man/Boy Love Association (NAMBLA) within the group. Spearheaded by conservative politicians, including Jesse Helms, the charges provoked IGLA to expel NAMBLA from the organization in hope of retaining its consultative status. That anti-gay outsiders instigated the purge of NAMBLA from IGLA is substantiated by the fact that NAMBLA had participated in IGLA without incident prior to the public attacks. The action was a result of a change in the group's communicative environment that "triggered attempts to define the collective more purely" (1997, 187).

Not all challenges to collective identity are launched by outsiders. As we have recounted, in the early days of VOTF the Church hierarchy and some lay Catholics tried to neutralize their change efforts by disqualifying them as faithful Catholics. A similar dynamic of contested membership among insiders occurred when the Michigan Womyn's Music Festival expelled transgender women from participation (Browne 2009; Gamson 1997). This challenge arose internally and was motivated by the goal of creating a safe space for "womyn-born womyn." In response to the expulsion, excluded trans women set up what came to be known as Camp Trans across the road from the festival.

According to Kath Browne (2009), the boundary dispute involving the admission of trans women was constitutive of the Womyn's Fest identity, rather than a challenge to it. In negotiating and articulating the reasons for the exclusion of trans women, the Womyn's Fest developed an identity as "womyn" in relation to women (the latter being a larger category that included both the trans women and the festival attendees). A significant aspect of the negotiations with Camp Trans involved acknowledging their commonality. In 2008, Lisa Vogel, the founder of the festival, issued a statement referring to Camp Trans as "sisters in struggle" and to all of them (womyn and trans women) as being "members of the greater queer community," even while patrolling the boundary that would exclude trans women. For Browne, the "paradoxes and juxtaposition of womyn's space and Camp Trans" was, in this sense, "productive."

Finally, events in a group's environment may indirectly provoke groups to reflect on their identity, even in the absence of, or in anticipation of, a direct challenge from either insiders or outsiders. In her case study of the dissemination of direct action tactics after the WTO protests in Seattle, Lesley Wood describes the significance of the 9/11 terrorist attacks.

The attacks and the confusion that followed 9/11 led to intense and emotional conversations. Both informal and formal, these conversations were partly attempts to answer questions like: "What do the 9/11 attacks mean for our tactics, identity, and strategy? What should we be doing now? Since the attacks, who are we? Who are we against . . . ?" (2012, 136)

Hoping to avoid alienating a shaken public or provoking a recently valorized police force, the global justice activists were grappling with ways to pursue their challenge to global capitalism while differentiating themselves from the 9/11 terrorists in the eyes of various audiences. Drawing that boundary changed not only their own sense of who they were, it also changed the tactics they were willing to employ. After one marcher burned an American flag at a post-9/11 protest, there were arguments about the appropriateness of that action. According to one account, the majority sentiment was, "This is not what we are about. This is not the message we want to send" (Wood 2012, 143).

Timing of Mobilization

The timing of mobilization and entrance into a group is also important for collective identity work, particularly distinct age, period, and cohort effects. As Nancy Whittier (1996) demonstrates through the history of feminist activism in Columbus, there are political generations that bring collective life experiences into organizations and become active within specific contexts. These generations are "comprised of individuals (of varying ages) who join a social movement during a given wave of protest" (1997, 762). Cohorts typically construct a shared sense of "we" based on their conditions of mobilization. Within a given cohort she further distinguishes microcohorts, which are "clusters of participants who enter a social movement within a year or two of each other and are shaped by the transformative experiences that differ because of subtle shifts in the political context" (ibid.). Cohort replacement, typical in movements, often produces changes in organizational forms and collective identities, injecting dynamism into a movement as these cohorts enter and exit within a shifting political environment. Additionally, she mentions that cohorts can be analyzed in terms of the age of the participants as well as the period of mobilization. Age groups bring with them a set of accumulated experiences analytically distinct from period and cohort effects.

Whittier illustrates these propositions by charting changes in collective identity and organizational births and deaths over the course of the feminist movement in Columbus from the late 1960s to the early 1990s. She analyzes the ways in which the fluctuation of cohorts created cohort conflict motivating these transformations. Her analytic framework can be applied readily to Ghaziani's studies of the gay and lesbian Washington, DC, marches and the transformation of the Princeton LGBTQ alliance. In both cases the movement of microcohorts in and out of activist groups brought significant changes to their strategies and tactics, organizational constitution, and construction of collective identity.

Whittier's analytic framework poses questions for the application of our approach to collective identity beyond our case of St. Erasmus VOTF. As we have detailed, the vast majority of these activists were roughly the same age and joined the chapter within a period of several months. Moreover, the group did not experience a succession of microcohorts, since it was unable to recruit significant numbers of new members over time. Instead, there was a slow attrition of members over time, leaving a core group that had been active since the chapter's inception.

Finally, as readers might have recognized, all of the above factors are beholden to the structural locations of members in the challenging group. We already have drawn on Benita Roth's (2004) examination of the rise of white feminists in the late 1960s and early 1970s. This is only a piece of her larger intersectional analysis of how African Americans and Latinas, facing distinct challenges because of race, forged "separate paths" to second-wave feminist activism. Likewise, in his analysis of the LGBTQ Washington, DC, marches, Ghaziani (2008) discusses the ways in which the organizing committees had to navigate racial and gender representations in their organization and presentation of collective identity. These examples could be replicated many times over as to how intersectional locations of members and subgroups add significant complexity to the ongoing processes of identity work among challenging groups and the larger movements of which they are a part.

The very homogeneous nature of the St. Erasmus VOTF chapter has not given us a vantage point by which we can pursue these questions with regard to our emergent model. As we have noted, the chapter members were entirely white, almost wholly senior citizens, and largely retirees with upper-middle-class professional backgrounds. Most had lived their formative years in white Catholic enclaves and as adults established themselves largely in the white, affluent suburbs that provided easy access to the parish in which they met. Among a more diverse group, however, structural location would likely affect members' emergent sense of temporality (given differences in experience) as well as their relational understandings of their places on the external and internal axes through which sameness and difference are constructed. Research on more diverse challenging groups should tease out these complexities.

Conclusion

Fifteen years is unusually long time for a small group like the St. Erasmus VOTF to persevere, particularly when confronting a powerful and generally intractable institution such as the Catholic Church. The dominant model of social movements holds some ready answers to this puzzle. Since most members were retired with grown children, they had the time to devote to the group. Coming from largely affluent backgrounds, professional lives, and a lifetime in the Church they have the financial wherewithal and secular and religious knowledge to facilitate the development of an activist habitus. Frequent and regular meetings produced strong and intimate networks enhancing endurance. In addition to these factors, the St. Erasmus VOTF was able to successfully construct and maintain a strong collective identity. They engaged in ongoing questioning and doubt about who they were and how they were to act. Doing so required that they continually manage a number of "crises" by restoring a tension between sameness and difference along the three axes of identity that we propose. Critical to their persistence, then, was that they recurrently returned to basic questions such as "Who are we as Catholics?", "What does this identity tell us about our faith and its practice?", and "How do we respond and move beyond betrayal given this identity?" In responding to these questions, they were able to sustain a sense of the group and its purpose despite the challenges they encountered.

In this chapter we have attempted to extend the model of collective identity to other social movement groups. While noting variations and complexities among groups, we claim that all groups construct a collective identity along these axes. The "identity trouble" a group experiences will occur in regard to issues of continuity–change, sameness–difference with outsiders, and sameness–difference among group members. Ironically, out of the countervailing pull of sameness and difference emerges something that feels solid, permanent, and abiding and this, in turn, becomes the basis for agency. By examining a number of case studies, we suggest factors that influence the type of identity work that might be necessary without specifying any particular sequence. Dynamism along each axis and in the relationship among them animates the process of identity; the capacity to regain a productive tension between sameness and difference ultimately determines whether a group will succeed.

Epilogue: Hearing Again

Either you had no purpose
Or the purpose is beyond the end you figured
And is altered in fulfillment. T. S. ELIOT, "LITTLE GIDDING"

I remember going through a conversation . . . before this whole thing had started. We started talking about the practices we had grown up with. You know, it's baloney. But then how much baloney? How far in do you dig? I annoy people. Because I'm a digger. And I said to these people, "How do you know that Jesus is not just Santa Claus without a suit?" And there's a long pause. And, as often happens, maybe a week later or a month later or something, the question comes back and I ask, "Why did I say that?" Because now I've got to think about it. And suddenly it becomes very clear. If there is no uncertainty, if you don't have doubt, then what you have is not faith. It's something else. THOMAS

The *Boston Globe* Spotlight team entitled their book about the sex abuse scandal *Betrayal*, a word that simply but powerfully captured the feeling of most members of VOTF at the time. It was indisputably a story of institutional betrayal. Yet, years later, it turns out it is also a story about trust and faith. The somewhat unexpected moral of the story is that it was not the betrayal by the Church hierarchy that shattered the trust of the Catholics we studied; the betrayal was instead the ground upon which their trust emerged and their faith deepened.

This claim seems to upend the taken-for-granted relationship between trust and betrayal. Trust is more typically cast as a casualty of betrayal rather than its consequence. Before the sex scandal, members of St. Erasmus VOTF never imagined the possibility that there could be widespread

139

sexual abuse of children by priests, nor could they fathom that the Church hierarchy would cover up such crimes. Because they did not imagine such a possibility, they could not *trust* that it would not occur. To trust is to proceed in the face of uncertainty; on the matter of the sexual abuse of children there was no uncertainty in the minds of most Catholics.[1]

This is not to say, however, that St. Erasmus VOTF members were not betrayed. Although the word is often coupled with trust, its etymology is closer to deceit and revelation, as a traitor might reveal information to an enemy or, more colloquially, our actions or words might "betray" some underlying truth.[2]

The sex scandal embodied both senses of the word: It revealed to the world a lie and a cover-up. It was at that moment of revelation that the future members of St. Erasmus VOTF faced a decision: to leave, or to stay faithful to the Church, only now with this horrible awareness of the unthinkable, and find a way to trust.

Initially, they began in 2002 by laying out a plan to "change the Church" into an institution that was trustworthy. Although there were differences of opinion about what these reforms would entail—greater accountability, transparency, and inclusion of lay Catholics in decision-making—they all focused on changing the institution. With time, these betrayed but faithful Catholics discovered that before they could change the Church they needed to change themselves. Trust is, at its base, an interactively generated relationship that depends not only on the trustworthiness of the recipient but also on the trustor's capacity to give or withhold trust (Barbalet 2009).

By definition, trust cannot be coerced or forced. It is given, and to be meaningful it must be given freely. "The capacity for refusal," John Hewitt writes, "lies at the heart of the human capacity for autonomy" (1989, 180). During most of the twentieth century the embeddedness of Catholic parish life made leaving the Church difficult and costly—socially, economically, and spiritually. While "refusing" the Church in this context was possible, it was improbable. By 2002 the possibility of leaving the Church—or quietly "lapsing"—carried considerably fewer costs or sacrifices. According to sociologist of religion Grace Davie, an observable trend has been from "an understanding of religion as a form of obligation to an increasing emphasis on 'consumption' or choosing. What until recently was simply imposed . . . or inherited . . . becomes instead a matter of personal choice" (2007, 30). Reflecting this trend, at the time of the scandal the members of St. Erasmus VOTF lived and worked in communities that were highly secularized. Many of their neighbors, friends, coworkers, and even family were not Catholic, and those who were would not have judged them harshly had they responded to the scandal by turning away from the Church. Indeed, it was precisely the possibility of refusal that made their staying meaningful in a way it would not have been in a less secularized and more obligatory time and place. Early on, the members of St. Erasmus VOTF were in fact frequently asked by friends, family, and coworkers why they did not just leave the Church when the abuse of power and sex was uncovered. Their shock and intense sense of betrayal by the Church would have warranted leaving, and it did for many in the archdiocese. That they did not leave and, even more, that they remained stubbornly committed to the Church was perhaps their boldest act of collective resistance and challenge.

The fact that St. Erasmus VOTFers could have refused, but did not; the fact that they exercised their autonomy by remaining in the Church may account for the fact that many of them reported an enhanced faith as a result of the sexual abuse scandal. Thomas put it more eloquently when he said, "If there is no uncertainty, if you don't have doubt, then what you have is not faith. It's something else." His words echo those of James Carroll, a major Catholic commentator and writer, when he describes an alternative to doubt and disillusionment and, in this case, betrayal.

> [W]e can retreat into fundamentalism, into the indifference of stark relativism, or into aggressive rejectionism. Or we can deliberately embrace what Paul Ricœur calls a "post-critical naiveté." Innocence is no virtue unless, after failure and disillusionment, it is chosen. Ricœur also calls this state of mind a "second naiveté," which implies a movement through criticism to a renewed appetite for the sacred traditions out of which we come, while implying that we are alive to its meaning in a radically different way—alive to its limits, and its corruptions as well. (2009, 313)

In the spring of 2017, as the attendance at meetings grew sparser, the remaining core members of St. Erasmus VOTF considered different and possibly divergent steps forward. They were once again calling on their faith to confront doubt and reconsider their project and its horizon. It is tempting, in light of their decision to disband, to ask, "How successful were they? What did they achieve?" Indeed, over the course of their fifteen-year run, the St. Erasmus VOTF chapter made progress toward their initial goals and aspirations. Survivors had been invited to talk to the group about their victimization and been given a compassionate audience. Members of VOTF had stood alongside survivors in public protest. And the group had provided financial support for those survivors who otherwise could not attend national conferences or afford therapy. The integrity of priests who spoke out against the hierarchy in the wake of the scandal or who simply served faithfully had been recognized and embraced by the group. Changes within the Church (the third plank) are harder to catalogue. Cardinal Law remained ensconced in the Vatican until his death, when he was given an elaborate and celebratory funeral. In general, the hierarchy has resisted the inclusion of lay voices in Church governance. Women cannot be ordained; priests must, with few exceptions, take a vow of celibacy. Indeed, their decision seems to affirm Peter McDonough's assessment that they were more like Pluto than Mars, that is, not really a social movement at all.

In this book, we chose to adopt a different perspective on challenging groups—one that renders questions about success or failure less salient and less interesting. Following Joseph Gusfield, we have asked instead, "What happened?" Rather than gauge success in terms of programmatic goals, we describe how a small group of people responded to a crisis of meaning, how their response generated new meanings, new values, and new identities. We chose to focus on effects rather than effectiveness.

In short, the scandal, or more specifically their response to it, offered these individuals a tragic opportunity for reconstituting themselves. VOTF's original purpose to "change the Church" was altered in its pursuit. To trust when there are good reasons not to, to stay committed when there are abundant reasons to leave, to have faith in the midst of uncertainty may in fact be the key accomplishments of Voice of the Faithful. Paradoxically, for many of the VOTF activists we met, the sexual abuse scandal and its aftermath strengthened their faith, intensified their Catholic identity, and expanded the scope of their participation within the Church. This renewal is due in large part to the fact that these Catholics interpreted and experienced their activism as an expression and practice of their faith. For even while it shocked their sacred universe, their participation in this community of challengers within brought them Ricœur's second naiveté.

142

Notes

1. Hebblethwaite 1984, 444. Soon after the second Vatican Council had begun, Pope John was diagnosed with terminal stomach cancer. He knew that he would not able to complete the reforms he envisioned in calling the council.
2. Bernard Law was archbishop of the archdiocese of Boston from 1984 to his resignation under pressure in 2002. For his role in the scandal see below.
3. Law used this phrase a number of times in his responses to the scandal. In responding to the revelations of serial predations by Father Paul Shanley and their cover-up, he wrote in a letter to the laity: "We are the Church. That 'we' must be never understood in an exclusive sense, however. It is not just 'We the Laity,' or 'We the Hierarchy,' or 'We the Clergy,' or 'We the Religious,' or 'We the Prophetic Voice.' It is all of us together" (*The Pilot*, May 24, 2002, 7). VOTF's use of the phrase can be seen as a dialogic appropriation to legitimize their standing.
4. Edyvean has since retired, while O'Connell became the judicial vicar and was recently promoted to the position of auxiliary bishop (*Globe*, June 3, 2016).
5. http://www.faithfulvoice.com/mondello1.htm.
6. By this time the dioceses of Bridgeport, CT; Portland, ME; Camden and Newark, NJ; Baker, OR; and Brooklyn and Rockville Center, NY, had all banned VOTF chapters (*Globe*, November 11, 2002).
7. Two years after Cardinal Law resigned, Pope John Paul II appointed him the archpriest of the Basilica di Santa Maria Maggiore in Rome. This appointment was interpreted by many in St. Erasmus VOTF as a recapitulation of the abuse of

power Cardinal Law perpetrated. Whereas he reassigned abusive priests to other parishes, the pope reassigned Cardinal Law to a prestigious position within the Church.

8. As Charles Curran observes, "Who carries out the social mission of the Church? The basic answer is simple—all baptized members of the Church. Catholic theology recognizes the bishops' oversight and teaching in the Church and its social mission. As overseers the bishops have a responsibility to make the whole Church recognize the theoretical and practical importance of the social mission. But individual Catholics, various movements, and institutions also exercise important leadership functions as regards the social mission of the Church" (2011, ix).

9. According to the Vatican, "the hierarchy within the body exercising authority in the Catholic Church is stipulated in the canon law of the Catholic Church. The Roman Catholic Church is led by the pope, who oversees the entire welfare of the church with the help of other leaders of the Church. The members of the administration of the Catholic Church are the pope, cardinals, archbishops, bishops, priests, and deacons. Every individual at each hierarchy level is assigned with overseeing specific functions of the church and has to coordinate with other leaders of the Church to lead the Catholic believers they are representing" (Vatican.com). When members of VOTF refer to the "hierarchy," they are generally referring to bishops, archbishops, cardinals, and the pope. Although almost all of the abusive clergy were priests, the members of VOTF often expressed their greatest anger at "the hierarchy."

CHAPTER ONE

1. The pragmatist John Dewey, reflecting on the human condition, observed, "If it is better to travel than to arrive, it is because traveling is a constant arriving, while arrival that precludes further traveling is most easily attained by going to sleep or dying" (1922, 282). In the same spirit we want to suggest an orientation to collective challenges that focuses on traveling as much as arriving.

2. At the same time, he acknowledges the difficulty of maintaining the sense of identity as process: "the word identity is semantically inseparable from the idea of permanence and is, perhaps, for this very reason, ill-suited to the processual analysis for which I am arguing" (1995, 46).

3. In a similar vein, Zygmunt Bauman claims that identity, "though ostensibly a noun, acts like a verb, albeit a strange one to be sure: it appears only in the future tense. Though all too often hypostasized as an attribute of a material entity, identity has the ontological status of a project and a postulate" (1996, 19).

4. Here we are offering a modified version of Hewitt's (1989) symbolic interactionist perspective on the self. David Snow (2013) places a similar emphasis

on the relational nature of social movement identity work but does not specify specific axes.

5. See for example Engel (1993), Owens (2008), Polletta (2006), and Somers (1994) for versions of this argument.

6. Snow and McAdam (2000) propose that identity work involves either convergence, in which individuals realize that their personal identities are congruent with a social movement, or construction, through which personal or movement identities need to be aligned consciously. We reconceptualize these as ongoing processes, both of which occur on the self–other axis.

7. As the feminist theorist Lorraine Code argues, "[K]nowing other people, precisely because of the fluctuations and contradictions of subjectivity, is an ongoing communicative, interpretive process. It can never be fixed or complete; any fixity . . . is at best a fixity of flux" (in Sampson 1993, 104).

8. For a somewhat parallel argument see Ghaziani 2008. We discuss this perspective in more detail in chapter 4.

9. Similarly, Polletta observes, "narrative's configuration of events over time makes them important to the construction and maintenance of individual and collective identity" (1998, 140; see also Ashmore, Deaux, and McLaughlin-Volpe 2004, 107).

10. Here we juxtapose an emphasis on narratives with Snow and McAdam's (2000) assertion that most identity work is accomplished through framing.

11. Stories provide the cultural framework for ongoing action and organization, by which novel events can be made familiar and through which the past, present, and future are tied together. Reflecting this quality of activism, Gary Alan Fine argues that "to establish a collective selfhood the past must be incorporated into the present, cementing the group's recall by emphasizing that to know and to narrate is to belong to the group" (2010, 365; see also Davis 2002; Gergen 2009; Eliasoph and Lichterman 2003; Owens 2008; Polletta 1998, 2002, 2006).

12. See also Ewick and Silbey (2003, 1341).

13. As we discuss later, the St. Erasmus VOTFers' narrative of being faithful Catholics was realized partly through the ritual aspects of their weekly meetings, starting with the VOTF opening prayer and a hymn. Grace Yurich (2009) uses a similar concept when she refers to the "concrete practices that embody stories." For related perspectives see Pennebaker and Banasik (1997) and Armstrong and Crage (2006).

14. See for explanations Davis (2002); Engel and Munger (2003); Ewick and Silbey (1995, 1998); Gergen (2009).

15. Similarly, Meredith McGuire suggests, "Lived religion is constituted by the practices people remember, share, enact, adopt, and create the 'stories out of which they live.' And it is constituted through practices by which people turn these 'stories' into everyday action" (2007, 197).

16. See Polletta (2006) for an account of how stories end with an ellipsis, which elicits further stories.

17. As Polletta notes, "External developments may discredit a dominant institutional story. Or external developments may heighten the tension between two institutional stories that once coexisted harmoniously" (2006, 17).

18. For a now classic institutionalist account of transposition see Clemens (1997).

19. As Albert Bandura observes, "People's beliefs in their collective efficacy influence the type of social future they seek to achieve, how much effort they put into it, and their endurance when collective efforts fail to produce quick results. The stronger they believe in their capabilities to effect social change the more actively they engage in collective efforts" (1999, 35).

20. Social psychologist Martijn van Zomeren and colleagues argue that collective identity and efficacy, as well as a sense of injustice, are related (van Zomeren et. al. 2004, 2008).

21. For a similar argument see Jasper (1997).

22. As Emirbayer and Mische likewise propose, "All social groups possess repertoires of stories that serve as temporal framing resources and that help define membership in a community (Carr 1986; Somers 1992); the degree of specificity and complexity with which futures are imagined is closely related to the salience of existing narratives and the 'careers' (White 1992) that they present as morally and practically acceptable" (1998, 989).

23. We note that St. Erasmus VOTFers focused on matters of collective identity not only because it was a matter of ontological security, but also because their circumstances as resourceful actors provided them the opportunity to do so. As a largely affluent group who were secure in other aspects of their lives, they had the habitus and material resources to mobilize and persevere in their project of being faithful Catholics that more marginalized groups often lack. Their marginality as Catholics growing up is an issue that we pursue in our analysis of collective identity.

PART TWO

1. http://www.catholic.org/featured/headline.php?ID=1143.

2. "Church Rises and Falls on Immigrant Tide," *New York Times*, September 22, 2015, A1.

3. Journalist reports of the scandal contain stark accounts by survivors of how their claims of abuse were either not believed or repressed by family members and Church authorities (D'Antonio 2013; Investigative Staff of the *Boston Globe* 2002). Survivors who spoke to the St. Erasmus chapter offered strikingly similar stories.

4. The dominant model, in its variations, implicitly conceptualizes power as secular, often organized in hierarchical structures of authority, and used or enacted in largely systemic and instrumental ways to produce distinctions of enduring difference between actors. Most analysts explicitly or implicitly employ state-centered models that incorporate these characteristics. Certainly the power exercised by Church hierarchy can be conceived in

institutional terms, and their handling of abusing priests, the cover-up, and their subsequent relations with VOTF and other change seekers can be viewed through this lens. Scholars have argued for a more multiinstitutional approach to power that broadens both the range of authority and challenges to it that merit scrutiny (Armstrong and Bernstein 2008). We seek to extend this approach by further reconceptualizing the bases of authority.

CHAPTER TWO

1. We find some parallels here with Jeffrey Olick's analyses of the politics of collective memory. He concludes, for example, that "the problem of collective memory is thus synonymous with the problem of collective identity" (2007, 188). Additionally, he argues that analytic focus should be on collective remembering as a relational "ongoing process of mediation rather than of storage and retrieval" (2007, 88).
2. For a parallel see Polletta's (2006) analysis of the narrative used by the student activists explaining their lunch counter sit-ins in Greensboro. Likewise, Arthur Frank maintains, "Movement stories that fabricate the group are fabricated; actions are planned to generate an already imagined story of those actions. Then a story is told that reconstructs what happened as spontaneous" (2012, 132). In addition, Robert Jansen (2007) notes that collective memory can be constructed through "mnemonic battles" with elites to determine legitimacy.
3. Olick (2007) argues that mnemonic practices are vital for a group's continuity.
4. Similarly, Nancy Whittier observes, "Discursive change entails telling new stories about the operation of institutions, challenging the legitimation of power and the production of identities that are part of the dominant discourse" (2002, 303).
5. As Holland et. al. (1998) emphasize, narratives are heuristics rather than set scripts. Through their characters and plots they provide the bases for the temporal and in situ improvisation required by ongoing activity.
6. As Melucci notes, collective identity is a "system of vectors in tension" (1996, 76).
7. As Arthur Frank suggests, "two stories are the beginning of *thinking*, as opposed to being caught up in one story. Two stories instigate dialogue" (2012, 152). Successor stories are necessary for collective actors to create reflexivity in the face of new challengers. As Owens (2008) poignantly demonstrates, holding fast to origin stories can facilitate the demise of a social movement.
8. In his relational perspective on identity (what he terms "relational being"), Kenneth Gergen argues that the process of identity exists in a relational flow. Identity is produced in "a process of relational flow in which there is both continuous movement toward constraint, on one hand, and an openness to the evolution of meaning on the other. In the process of relational

flow, we generate durable meaning together in local conditions, but in doing so continuously innovate in ways that are sensitive to the multiplicity of relationships in which we are engaged" (2009, 46).

9. As we emphasize elsewhere, the narrative process and the identity work done through it are dialogic. See also Frank (2012), Holland et. al. (1998), and Olick (2007).

10. Additionally, Frank observes that storytelling is a process of "reassembly," by which fragments of past stories are pieced together in slightly different form (2012, 14–15, 83).

11. As Frank (2012), Polletta (2006), and others observe, we often do not create these stories *de nouveau* but draw on a repertoire of standard plots that have collective intelligibility.

12. As Holland et. al. suggest, a key part of identity is a "history-in-person": "One's history-in-person is the sediment from past experiences upon which one improvises, using the cultural resources available, in response to subject positions afforded one in the present" (1998, 18). Dramatic events such as the *Globe* revelations can wash away this "sediment," leaving a person on uncertain ontological ground.

13. This is another attribute of our case that differentiates it from the theory of moral shock.

14. As Helena Flam (2005) notes in her theoretical approach to emotions and social movements, some emotions among challenging groups can be "unruly" and are not easily tamed by "feeling rules" constructed by the group. In these initial meetings at the parish, participants experienced such unruliness, but as they settled on the main planks of the group they also succeeded in creating an affective structure.

15. Deborah Gould makes the case that "affective states can shake one out of deeply grooved patterns of thinking and feeling and allow new imaginings. However, as they develop movements 'make sense' of affective states and authorize selected feelings and actions while downplaying and even invalidating others" (2009, 27–28).

16. Over the years there has been an expanding literature on emotions and social movements (for example, see Flam and King [2005]; Goodwin [1997]; Goodwin, Jasper, and Polletta [2001]; Gould [2009]; Jasper [2011]). This research predominantly has focused on structured and longer-term affective states that are tied to enduring cognitive dimensions of collective action. In other words, they focus on specific emotions, such as anger or hope, as an ongoing impetus for mobilization paired with cognitive and organizational processes. Largely neglected in this literature are the ways in which challengers in their ongoing efforts hold and must manage contradictory emotions. This is particularly the case for challengers within.

17. Symbolically the donation serves multiple purposes. It demonstrates that the members are faithful Catholics of the parish and not set apart from it. In addition, VOTF in its early years had set up a separate fund for giving to

Catholic Charities to circumvent the annual call for giving by the Boston Archdiocese and express their dissatisfaction with the hierarchy. In doing so, they sought to demonstrate their independent agency. The St. Erasmus chapter's gift could be seen in parallel fashion.

18. For an account of this transformation, see O'Connor (1998).

19. Loretta's secular autobiography also prominently featured a story of how she overcame gender discrimination in a major insurance and financial services corporation.

CHAPTER THREE

1. See Einwohner, Reger, and Myers (2008).

2. Michael Paulson, "Bishop Bans Group from Meetings at Parish," *Boston Globe*, October 1, 2002.

3. As Fine notes, "Who one is, and also who one imagines that one is, depends on those who surround one and those spaces and scenes in which one participates" (2012a, 162).

4. Places can also function to define a group by demarcating those zones to which the group is denied access, or by allowing for disruptions in conventional spatial practices. What Rob Shields calls social spatialization can often involve using space to resist the restrictions of one's social status by occupying or "reterritorializing" space. When the Boston archdiocese announced plans to close some parishes in 2004, it met with considerable resistance from some parishioners, and five parishes responded by occupying their churches. Ultimately the archdiocese scaled back this consolidation plan. See Seitz 2011.

5. Wilde highlights some of the many significant changes as follows:

> [T]he Roman Catholic Church relinquished its claim to be the one true church, and with it abdicated claims to power in relation to nation-states, by declaring that the only just form of government was one under which people were free to worship as they pleased. The Council relaxed dietary restrictions and requirements regarding confession and attire for the laity, eliminated Latin mass, and forever changed the character and identities of Roman Catholic nuns and brothers—and their orders. Most importantly, Vatican II changed the way in which the Church understood itself, as its identity went from being a hierarchical authority to a church conceived as the people of God. (2007, 1)

Vatican II became a central part of the process of narrating the identity of St. Erasmus VOTFers.

6. See for example Baggett (2008, 15–18); Dillon (1999, 47–51); and Groome (2002, 118, 156–57).

7. Óscar Romero was the archbishop of El Salvador who was transformed by his ascension to the post in 1977 from a "safe" traditionalist to an advocate

for the poor and a critic of the state. He called on members of the military to search their consciences when it came to participating in the repression of leftists and the battles to suppress a popular rebellion. He was assassinated in March 1980 because of his outspokenness. As Sharon Erickson Nepstad (2004) notes, his fate became a popular "martyr story" that provided narrative impetus to recruit Central American peace activists.

8. St. Erasmus members were partly aware of the importance of myth in their own religiosity. At one event about the reflection on and meaning of Christmas just prior to the holiday, one presenter, Jeremy, pointed to the consequence of such stories in their lives. In discussing the story of St. Nicholas of Turkey he explained the value of myth for society, the strength it provides in constructing worldviews, society's origins, identity, customs, and behaviors. A participant at one of our discussion tables followed with a comment that it was important for VOTF to look at these stories anew for the spiritual bases of the Church.

9. As Fine and Harrington note, "Through the narration of experience, meaningful group events radiate outward from the locus of interactions" (2004, 345).

10. As Michele Dillon observes,

> The redrawing of interpretive authority validated an understanding of religious identity derived from a more egalitarian, communal sense of church ownership rather than from the church hierarchy's universal definitions alone. . . . The respondents' doctrinal "knowledge" supports their efforts to dismantle, rather than maintain, the church's exclusionary boundaries. In their view, they cannot be Catholic without contesting the inegalitarian institutional practices justified by the hierarchy. (1999, 48, 1776)

Cathy Holtmann suggests that religious identities are "fluid and changing in order to adapt to life's circumstances," and that Vatican II provided women with a greater sense of agency in this regard (2011, 144).

11. For parallel examinations of appropriation of ritual by Catholic Worker groups, see James V. Spickard (2005) and Grace Yukich (2010). As the latter notes, through ritual practices Workers "create a distinctive identity as Catholics but not 'Catholic,'" i.e., bound to the faith but not to the traditional and hierarchical institution (184).

12. The VOTF prayer is as follows:

> For all victims of sexual abuse by Roman Catholic priests,
> we pray always for you.
> We mean to be agents of your healing.
>
> Response: We are the Church; we are the Body of Christ.
> Hear us, Christ our strength and salvation,
> help us all.

For all our brothers and sisters in faith,
as we struggle to become the Spirit-filled Church we are called to be,
move us to accept the challenges of reform that are demanded by today's
injustices.

Response: We are the Church; we are the Body of Christ.
Hear us, Christ our truth and salvation,
help us all.

For all bishops of the Roman Catholic Church,
that their hearts and minds be opened to the Church's call to genuine
holiness and truth,
a call to inclusion and collaboration with the faithful.

Response: We are the Church; we are the Body of Christ.
Hear us, Christ our strength and salvation,
help us all.

For all who minister in the name of Jesus Christ,
and especially for our Roman Catholic priests,
we pray for your continued faithfulness to the Gospel and to the voice of
the faithful.

Response: We are the Church; we are the Body of Christ.
Hear us, Christ our strength and salvation,
help us all.

We are the Church; we are the Body of Christ.
Strengthen us, fill us with wisdom,
lead us to holy action in building up your reign.
Help us to respect our voice and the voices of all the faithful.

Response: We are your Church; we are the Body of Christ.
Hear us, Christ our true life and salvation.
Amen.

13. As Armstrong and Crage note, "Embedding commemorative ritual in the recurring, routine activities of a group also promotes survival (e.g., designating a day each year for commemoration). Ritual provides the opportunity to rehearse memories" (2006, 727).

14. In a parallel manner, Baggett suggests that Church teachings and practices together provide the sense of serious reverence in which Catholics invest themselves (2008, 231).

15. For a similar phenomenological perspective, see Bender (2003) on lived religion.

16. During the first picnic we attended, the auxiliary bishop arrived, to the delight of a number of the members. They made him comfortable and a little while later made it a point of introducing us as sociologists studying

the group. The bishop quipped humorously but with a tinge of anxiety, "Should I get a lawyer now?"

17. See also Ecklund (2005, 2006) and Holtmann (2011).

18. See the classic description of this in Orsi (1985). In his history of Boston Catholicism, O'Toole notes that women in the mid-twentieth century were viewed primarily as the transmitters of the faith (2008, 148).

CHAPTER FOUR

1. Cristina Flesher Fominaya observes, "I would argue that some movements, including the global justice movement, understand and even explicitly define their collective identity in terms of diversity, heterogeneity, and inclusivity" (2010b, 399).

2. "Unlike strict consensus, the assumption here is that difference is an unavoidable element of solidarity. Group unity comes from recognizing the legitimacy of different opinions as well as shared ones. . . . Solidarity is created through the process of decision-making, not its endpoint" (210).

3. In regards to the internal groups that emerged around each of these three planks, it is important to note that each member's group affiliation with and allegiance to the various working groups was neither exclusive nor total. Some people straddled different groups, endorsing two or more goals equally; others were more exclusively committed to one over the other two. We are, in other words, not describing individuals, but the groups to which they were variously committed.

4. Indeed, during her fall 2007 talk, she noted that attempts by the national organization to delineate a set agenda had been "trying" and that at the present time there was no need for any additional consensus.

5. Here we can find some parallels to Stephen Hart's (2001) work on how progressive groups can be inhibited by the type of discourse through which they conduct their relations. Hart argues that groups either adopted "constrained discourses" (those that place off-limits larger questions of politics to maintain cohesion) or "expansive" ones (those that offer a means of discussing a group's transcendent values). The former also constrain the ways in which members can inhibit group dynamism.

6. Thomas casually discussed the early steering committee meetings with one of us one evening. Without going into detail he mentioned that in one of the formative meetings a small group had tried to take control of the chapter to pursue their agenda and were overridden by the others present.

7. Pam Belluck, "Catholic Lay Group Tests a Strategy Change," *New York Times,* June 24, 2007.

8. As Blee (2012) argues, while small activist groups establish their organizational process, structure, and guiding principles early, events can create a break in their assumed continuity, possibly leading to self-reflective transformation.

CHAPTER FIVE

1. In their critique of the concept of identity and cognate terms, Brubaker and Cooper refer to this contradiction: "They have been used to address the perennial philosophical problems of permanence amidst manifest change, and of unity amidst manifest diversity" (2000, 2).
2. Ghaziani refers to the Pride Alliance as the "local LBGT" student group. By adopting an earlier name, Ghaziani implicitly recognizes the communicative ambiguity of an identity-muting name like "Pride Alliance."
3. Similarly, one of the groups Blee studied, New Army of Revolution, was conceived when its founder saw "President Bush's reelection as an opportunity to build a progressive movement in Pittsburgh" (2012, 20). Much like Stonewall, the "spark" did not represent a rupture so much as an opportunity to build on existing projects to the extent that it constituted a continuation of the group's trajectory. The origin was a strategic choice to build upon events, rather than a temporal crisis of identity.

EPILOGUE

1. "This problem of time [attempting to make certain an unknowable future] is bridged by trust, paid ahead of time as an advance on success" (Luhmann 1979, 25).
2. The etymology is as follows: early thirteenth century, "prove false, violate by unfaithfulness"; ca. 1300, *bitrayen*, "deliver or expose to the power of an enemy by treachery," also "mislead, deceive, delude," from *be-* + obsolete Middle English *tray*, from Old French *traine* "betrayal, deception, deceit," from *trair* (Modern French *trahir*) "betray, deceive," from Latin *tradere* "hand over," from *trans* "across" + *dare* "to give" (from PIE root **do-* "to give"). On-line Etymology Dictionary (www.etymonline.com).

Bibliography

Abbott, Andrew. 2001. *Time Matters: On Theory and Method.* Chicago: University of Chicago Press.

Amenta, Edwin, Neal Caren, Elizabeth Chiarello, and Yang Su. 2010. "The Political Consequences of Social Movements." *Annual Review of Sociology* 36:287–307.

Ammerman, Nancy T. 2003. "Religious Identities and Religious Institutions." In *Handbook of the Sociology of Religion,* edited by Michele Dillon, 207–24. Cambridge: Cambridge University Press.

Andrews, Kenneth T., Marshall Ganz, Matthew Baggetta, Hahrie Han, and Chaeyoon Lim. 2010. "Leadership, Membership, and Voice: Civic Associations That Work." *American Journal of Sociology* 115 (4): 1191–242.

Armstrong, Elizabeth A., and Mary Bernstein. 2008. "Culture, Power, and Institutions: A Multi-Institutional Politics Approach to Social Movements." *Sociological Theory* 26 (1): 74–99.

Armstrong, Elizabeth A., and Suzanna M. Crage. 2006. "Movements and Memory: The Making of the Stonewall Myth." *American Sociological Review* 71 (5): 724–51.

Ashmore, Richard D., Kay Deaux, and Tracy McLaughlin-Volpe. 2004. "An Organizing Framework for Collective Identity: Articulation and Significance of Multidimensionality." *Psychological Bulletin* 130 (1) (Jan 2004): 80–114.

Baggett, Jerome P. 2008. *Sense of the Faithful: How American Catholics Live Their Faith.* Oxford: Oxford University Press.

Banaszak, Lee. 2010. *The Women's Movement Inside and Outside the State.* New York: Cambridge University Press.

Bandura, Alan. 1999. "Exercise of Personal and Collective Efficacy in Changing Societies." In *Self Efficacy in Changing Societies,* 1–45. Cambridge: Cambridge University Press.

Barbalet, Jack. 2009. "A Characterization of Trust, and Its Consequences." *Theory and Society* 38 (4): 367–82.

Bauman, Zygmunt. 1996. "From Pilgrim to Tourist—or a Short History of Identity." In *Questions of Cultural Identity*, edited by Stuart Hall and Paul du Gay, 18–36. London: Sage Publications.

Bellah, Robert, et al. 1985. *Habits of the Heart: Individualism and Commitment in American Life*. Berkeley: University of California Press.

Bender, Courtney. 2003. *Heaven's Kitchen: Living Religion at God's Love We Deliver*. Chicago: University of Chicago Press.

Berger, Peter, and Thomas Luckmann. 1966. *The Social Construction of Reality: A Treatise on the Sociology of Knowledge*. Garden City, NY: Doubleday.

Bernstein, Mary. 2005. "Identity Politics." *Annual Review of Sociology* 31:47–74.

———. 2008. "The Analytic Dimensions of Identity: A Political Identity Framework." In *Identity Work in Social Movements*, edited by Jo Reger, Rachel L. Einwohner, and Daniel J. Myers, 277–301. Minneapolis: University of Minnesota Press.

Blee, Kathleen. 2002. *Inside Organized Racism: Women in the Hate Movement*. Berkeley: University of California Press.

———. 2012. *Democracy in the Making: How Activist Groups Form*. New York: Oxford University Press.

———. 2013. "How Options Disappear: Causality and Emergence in Grassroots Activist Groups." *American Journal of Sociology* 119 (3): 655–81.

Braunstein, Ruth. 2012. "Storytelling in Liberal Religious Advocacy." *Journal for the Scientific Study of Religion* 51 (1): 110–27.

Browne, Kath. 2009. "Womyn's Separatist Spaces: Rethinking Spaces of Difference and Exclusion." *Transactions of the Institute of British Geographers*, n.s., 34 (4): 541–56.

Brubaker, Rogers and Frederick Cooper. 2000. "Beyond Identity." *Theory and Society* 29 (1): 1–47.

Bruce, Tricia Colleen. 2011. *Faithful Revolution: How Voice of the Faithful Is Changing the Church*. Oxford: Oxford University Press.

Carmella, Angela C. 2001. "A Catholic View of Law and Justice." In *Christian Perspectives on Legal Thought*, edited by Michael W. McConnell, Robert F. Cochran Jr., and Angela C. Carmella, 255–76. New Haven: Yale.

Carroll, James. 2009. *Practicing Catholic*. Boston: Houghton, Mifflin, Harcourt.

Clemens, Elisabeth S. 1997. *The People's Lobby: Organizational Innovation and the Rise of Interest Group Politics in the United States, 1890–1925*. Chicago: University of Chicago Press.

Crossley, Nick. 2003. "From Reproduction to Transformation: Social Movement Fields and the Radical Habitus." *Theory, Culture and Society* 20 (6): 43–68.

———. 2004. "Phenomenology, Structuralism and History: Merleau-Ponty's Social Theory." *Theoria* 103:88–121.

Curran, Charles E. 2011. *The Social Mission of the US Catholic Church*. Washington, DC: Georgetown University Press.

D'Antonio, Michael. 2013. *Mortal Sins: Sex, Crime, and the Ear of Catholic Scandal*. New York: Thomas Dunn Books.

D'Antonio, William V., James D. Davidson, Dean R. Hoge, and Mary L. Gauthier. 2007. *American Catholics Today: New Realities of Their Faith and Their Church.* Lanham: Sheen & Ward.

D'Antonio, William V., James D. Davidson, Dean R. Hoge, and Katherine Meyer. 2001. *American Catholics: Gender, Generation and Commitment.* Walnut Creek: AltaMira.

D'Antonio, William V., Michelle Dillon, and Mary L. Gauthier. 2013. *American Catholics in Transition.* Lanham, MD: Rowman & Littlefield.

D'Antonio, William V., and Anthony Pogorelc, eds. 2007. *Voices of the Faithful: Loyal Catholics Striving for Change.* New York: Herder & Herder.

Davie, Grace. 2007. "Vicarious Religion: A Methodological Challenge." In *Everyday Religion: Observing Modern Religious Lives,* edited by Nancy T. Ammerman, 21–35. New York: Oxford University Press.

Davis, Joseph E. 2002. "Narrative and Social Movements: The Power of Stories." In *Stories of Change: Narrative and Social Movements,* edited by Joseph E. Davis, 3–29. Chicago: University of Chicago Press.

della Porta, Donatella. 1995. *Social Movements, Political Violence and the State: A Comparative Analysis of Italy and Germany.* Cambridge: Cambridge University Press.

Densmore, Dana. 1971. "On Unity." *No More Fun and Games: A Journal of Female Liberation* 5:52–62.

Dewey, John. 1922. *Human Nature and Conduct: An Introduction to Social Psychology.* New York: The Modern Library.

Dillon, Michele. 1999. *Catholic Identity: Balancing Reason, Faith, and Power.* Cambridge: Cambridge University Press.

Echols, Alice. 1989. *Daring to Be Bad: Radical Feminism in America, 1967–1975.* Minneapolis: University of Minnesota Press.

Ecklund, Elaine H. 2005. "Different Identity Accounts for Catholic Women." *Review of Religious Research* 47 (2): 135–49.

———. 2006. "Organizational Culture and Women's Leadership: A Study of Six Catholic Parishes." *Sociology of Religion* 67 (1): 81–98.

Einwohner, Rachel L., Jo Reger, and Daniel J. Myers. 2008. "Introduction: Identity Work, Sameness and Difference in Social Movements." In *Identity Work in Social Movements,* edited by Jo Reger, Rachel L. Einwohner, and Daniel J. Myers, 1–17. Minneapolis: University of Minnesota Press.

Eliasoph, Nina. 1998. *Avoiding Politics: How Americans Produce Apathy in Everyday Life.* Cambridge: Cambridge University Press.

Eliasoph, Nina, and Paul Lichterman. 2003. "Culture in Interaction." *American Journal of Sociology* 108 (4): 735–94.

Emirbayer, Mustafa, and Ann Mische. 1998. "What is Agency?" *American Journal of Sociology* 102 (4): 962–1023.

Engel, David M. 1993. "Origin Myths: Narratives of Authority, Resistance, Disability, and Law." *Law & Society Review* 27 (4): 785–826.

Engel, David M., and Frank W. Munger 2003. *Rights of Inclusion: Law and Identity in the Life Stories of Americans with Disabilities.* Chicago: University of Chicago Press.

Erikson, Kai. 1976. *Everything in Its Path: Destruction of Community in the Buffalo Creek Flood*. New York: Simon & Schuster.

Ewick, Patricia, and Susan S. Silbey. 1995. "Subversive Stories and Hegemonic Tales: Toward a Sociology of Narrative." *Law & Society Review* 29 (2): 197–226

———. 1998. *The Common Place of Law: Stories of Everyday Life*. Chicago: University of Chicago Press.

———. 2003. "Narrating Social Structure: Stories of Resistance to Legal Authority." *American Journal of Sociology* 108 (6): 1328–72.

Fantasia, Rick. 1988. *Cultures of Solidarity: Consciousness, Action, and Contemporary American Workers*. Berkeley: University of California Press.

Fine, Gary Alan. 2010. "The Sociology of the Local: Action and Its Publics." *Sociological Theory* 28 (4): 355–76.

———. 2012a. "Group Culture and the Interaction Order: Local Sociology on the Meso-Level." *Annual Review of Sociology* 38:159–79.

———. 2012b. *Tiny Publics: A Theory of Group Action and Culture*. New York: Russell Sage Foundation.

Fine, Gary Alan, and Brooke Harrington. 2004. "Tiny Publics: Small Groups and Civil Society." *Sociological Theory* 22 (3): 341–56.

Flam, Helena. 2005. "Emotions' Map: A Research Agenda." In *Emotions and Social Movements*, edited by Helena Flam and Debra King, 19–40. London: Routledge.

Flam, Helena, and Debra King. 2005. "Introduction." In *Emotions and Social Movements*, edited by Helena Flam and Debra King., 1–18. London: Routledge.

Flesher Fominaya, Cristina. 2010a. "Collective Identity in Social Movements: Central Concepts and Debates." *Sociology Compass* 4 (6): 393–404.

———. 2010b. "Creating Cohesion from Diversity: The Challenge of Collective Identity Formation in the Global Justice Movement." *Sociological Inquiry* 80 (3): 377–404.

Foucault, Michel. 1994. "'*Omnes et Singulatim*': Toward a Critique of Political Reason." In *Michel Foucault: Power. Essential Works of Foucault 1954–1984*, vol. 3, edited by James D. Faubion, 298–325. New York: The New Press.

———. 2007. *Security, Territory, Population: Lectures at the Collège de France 1977–1978*. Edited by Michel Senellart. Translated by Graham Burchell. New York: Picador.

France, David. 2004. *Our Fathers: The Secret Life of the Catholic Church in the Age of Scandal*. New York: Broadway.

Frank, Arthur. 2012. *Letting Stories Breathe: A Socio-narratology*. Chicago: University of Chicago Press.

Freeman, Jo. 1975. *The Politics of Women's Liberation: A Case Study of an Emerging Social Movement and Its Relation to the Policy Process*. New York: David McKay.

Gamson, Joshua. 1995. "Must Identity Movements Self Destruct? A Queer Dilemma." *Social Problems* 42 (3): 390–407.

———. 1997. "Messages of Exclusion: Gender, Movements, and Symbolic Boundaries." *Gender and Society* 11 (2): 178–99.

Gamson, William A. 1990. *The Strategy of Social Protest*. 2nd ed. Belmont, CA: Wadsworth.

———. 1992. "The Social Psychology of Collective Action." In *Frontiers in Social Movement Theory*, edited by Aldon D. Morris and Carol McGlung Mueller, 53–76. New Haven: Yale University Press.

———. 2007. "The Virtues of Loyalty." In *Voices of the Faithful: Loyal Catholics Striving for Change*, edited by William D. D'Antonio and Anthony Pogorelc, 147–55. New York: Herder & Herder.

Ganz, Marshall. 2000. "Resources and Resourcefulness: Strategic Capacity in the Unionization of California Agriculture, 1959–1966." *American Journal of Sociology* 105 (4): 1003–62.

Gergen, Kenneth, 2005. "Narrative, Moral Identity and Historical Consciousness: A Social Constructionist Account." In *Narration, Identity, and Historical Consciousness*, edited by Jürgen Straub, 99–119. New York: Berghahn Books.

———. 2009. *Relational Being: Beyond Self and Community*. Oxford: Oxford University Press.

Gergen, Kenneth, and Mary Gergen. 1997. "Narratives of the Self." In *Memory, Identity, Community: The Idea of Narrative in the Human Sciences*, edited by Lewis P Hinchman and Sandra K. Hinchman, 161–84. Albany: SUNY Press.

Ghaziani, Amin. 2008. *The Dividends of Dissent: How Conflict and Culture Work in Lesbian and Gay Marches in Washington*. Chicago: University of Chicago Press.

———. 2011. "Post-Gay Collective Identity Construction." *Social Problems* 58 (1): 99–125.

Giddens, Anthony. 1984. *The Constitution of Society*. Cambridge: Polity.

———. 1991. *Modernity and Self-Identity*. Stanford: Stanford University Press.

Gitlin, Todd. 1987. *The Sixties: Years of Hope, Days of Rage*. New York: Bantam.

Giugni, Marco, Doug McAdam, and Charles Tilly, eds. 1999. *How Social Movements Matter: Theoretical and Comparative Studies on the Consequences of Social Movements*. Minneapolis: University of Minnesota Press.

Goldfarb, Jeffrey. 2006. *The Politics of Small Things: The Powers of the Powerless in Dark Times*. Chicago: University of Chicago Press.

Goodwin, Jeff. 1997. "The Libidinal Constitution of a High-Risk Social Movement: Affectual Ties and Solidarity in the Huk Rebellion, 1946–1954." *American Sociological Review* 62 (1): 53–69.

Goodwin, Jeff, and James M. Jasper, eds. 2004. *Rethinking Social Movements: Structure, Meaning, and Emotion*. Lanham, MD: Rowman & Littlefield.

Goodwin, Jeff, James M. Jasper, and Francesca Polletta. 2001. *Passionate Politics: Emotions and Social Movements*. Chicago: University of Chicago Press.

Gould, Deborah B. 2009. *Moving Politics: Emotion and ACT UP's Fight Against AIDS*. Chicago: University of Chicago Press.

Gray, Mark M., and Paul M. Perl. 2006. "Catholic Reactions to the News of Sexual Abuse Cases Involving Clergy." Center for Applied Research in the Apostolate. Georgetown University. April.

Greeley, Andrew. 2000. *The Catholic Imagination*. Berkeley: University of California Press.

Groome, Thomas H. 2002. *What Makes Us Catholic: Eight Gifts for Life*. San Francisco: HarperCollins.

Gutierrez, Betzaluz, Jennifer Howard-Grenville, and Maureen A. Scully. 2010. "The Faithful Rise Up: Split Identification and an Unlikely Change in Effort." *Academy of Management Journal* 53 (4): 673–99.

Gusfield, Joseph R. 1981. "Social Movements and Social Change: Perspectives of Linearity and Fluidity." *Research in Social Movements, Conflict, and Change* 4:317–37.

Hart, Stephen. 2001. *Cultural Dilemmas of Progressive Politics: Styles of Engagement among Grassroots Activists*. Chicago: University of Chicago Press.

Hebblethwaite, Peter. 1984. *John XXIII: Pope of the Council*. London: Geoffrey Chapman.

Hewitt, John P. 1989. *Dilemmas of the American Self*. Philadelphia: Temple University Press.

Hirschman, Albert O. 1982. *Shifting Involvements: Private Interest and Public Action*. Princeton: Princeton University Press.

Holland, Dorothy, William Lachicotte Jr., Debra Skinner, and Carole Cain. 1998. *Identity and Agency in Cultural Worlds*. Cambridge, MA: Harvard University Press.

Holtmann, Cathy. 2011. "Workers in the Vineyard: Catholic Women and Social Action." In *Religion, Spirituality and Everyday Practice*, edited by G. Giordan and W. H. Swatos Jr., 141–52. New York: Springer.

Hornsby-Smith, Michael. 2006. *An Introduction to Catholic Social Thought*. Cambridge: Cambridge University Press.

Hunt, Scott A., Robert D. Benford, and David A. Snow. 1994. "Identity Fields: Framing Processes and the Social Construction of Movement Identities." In *New Social Movements: From Ideology to Identity*, edited by Enrique Larana, Hank Johnston, and Joseph R. Gusfield, 185–208. Philadelphia: Temple University Press.

Investigative Staff of the *Boston Globe*. 2002. *Betrayal: The Crisis in the Catholic Church*. Boston: Little, Brown & Co.

Jansen, Robert S. 2007. "Resurrection and Appropriation: Reputational Trajectories, Memory Work, and the Political Use of Historical Figures." *American Journal of Sociology* 112 (4): 953–1007.

Jasper, James M. 1997. *The Art of Moral Protest*. Chicago: University of Chicago Press.

———. 2004. "A Strategic Approach to Collective Action: Looking for Agency in Social Movement Choices." *Mobilization* 9 (1): 1–16.

———. 2011. "Emotions and Social Movements: Twenty Years of Theory and Research." *Annual Review of Sociology* 37:285–303.

———. 2015a. "Introduction: The Identity Dilemma, Social Movements, and Contested Identity." In *The Identity Dilemma: Social Movements and Collective*

Identity, edited by Aidan McGarry and James M. Jasper, 1–41. Philadelphia: Temple University Press.

———. 2015b. "Introduction: Playing the Game." In *Players and Arenas: The Interactive Dynamics of Protest*, edited by James M. Jasper and Jan Willem Duyvendak, 9–32. Amsterdam: Amsterdam University Press.

Jasper, James M., and Jane D. Poulsen. 2005. "Recruiting Strangers and Friends: Moral Shocks and Social Networks in Animal Rights and Anti-Nuclear Protests." *Social Problems* 42 (4): 493–512.

Joas, Hans. 1996. *The Creativity of Action*. Translated by Jeremy Gaines and Paul Keast. Chicago: University of Chicago Press.

Joas, Hans, and Wolfgang Knöbel. 2009. *Social Theory: Twenty Introductory Lectures*. Translated by Alex Skinner. Cambridge: Cambridge University Press.

Juris, Jeffrey S. 2008. *Networking Futures: The Movements Against Corporate Globalization*. Durham: Duke University Press.

———. 2012 "Reflections on #Occupy Everywhere: Social Media, Public Space, and Emerging Logics of Aggregation." *American Ethnologist* 39 (2): 259–79.

Katz, Jack. 1988. *Seductions of Crime: Moral and Sensual Attractions in Doing Evil*. New York: Basic.

Katzenstein, Mary Fainsod. 1998. *Faithful and Fearless: Moving Feminist Protest Inside the Church and the Military*. Princeton: Princeton University Press.

Kertzer, David I. 1988. *Ritual, Politics & Power*. New Haven: Yale University Press.

King, Brayden G., and Sarah A. Soule. 2007. "Social Movements as Extra-institutional Entrepreneurs: The Effect of Protests on Stock Price Returns." *Administrative Science Quarterly* 52 (3): 413–42.

Kretschmer, Kelsy. 2009. "Contested Loyalties: Dissident Identity Organizations, Institutions and Social Movements." *Sociological Perspectives* 52 (4): 433–54.

Kurtz, Sharon. 2002. *Workplace Justice: Organizing Multi-Identity Movements*. Minneapolis: University of Minnesota Press.

Lampedusa, Giuseppe Tomasi di. 1963. *The Leopard*. Translated by Archibald Colquhoun. London: Fontana.

Leach, Darcy K. 2009. "An Elusive 'We': Antidogmatism, Democratic Practice, and the Contradictory Identity of the German Autonomen." *American Behavioral Scientist* 52 (7): 1042–68.

Leitz, Lisa. 2011. "Oppositional Identities: The Military Peace Movement's Challenge to Pro-Iraq War Frames." *Social Problems* 58 (2): 235–56.

Leming, Laura M. 2006. "Church as Contested Terrain: Voice of the Faithful and Religious Agency." *Review of Religious Research* 48 (1): 56–71.

Lichterman, Paul. 1999. "Talking Identity in the Public Sphere: Broad Visions and Small Spaces in Sexual Identity Politics." *Theory & Society* 28 (1): 101–41.

———. 2005. *Elusive Togetherness: Church Groups Trying to Bridge America's Divisions*. Princeton: Princeton University Press.

Loveland, Matthew T., and Margaret Ksander. 2014. "Shepherds and Sheep: Parish Reconfiguration, Authority, and Activism in a Catholic Diocese." *Review of Religious Research* 56:443–65.

Luhmann, Niklas. 1979. *Trust and Power.* New York: Wiley.

McAdam, Doug, and Hilary Schaffer Boudet. 2012. *Putting Movements in Their Place: Explaining Opposition to Energy Projects in the United States, 2000–2005.* Cambridge: Cambridge University Press.

McAdam, Doug, Sidney Tarrow, and Charles Tilly. 2001. *Dynamics of Contention.* Cambridge: Cambridge University Press.

McDonough, Peter. 2013. *The Catholic Labyrinth: Power, Apathy and a Passion for Reform in the American Church.* Oxford: Oxford University Press.

McGuire, Meredith. 2007. "Embodied Practices: Negotiation and Resistance." In *Everyday Religion: Observing Modern Religious Lives,* edited by Nancy T. Ammerman, 187–200. New York: Oxford University Press.

Mead, George Herbert. 1934. *The Philosophy of the Present.* Edited by Arthur E. Murray. Chicago: Open Court Publishing Company.

Melucci, Alberto. 1995. "The Process of Collective Identity." In *Social Movements and Culture,* edited by Hank Johnston and Bert Klandermans, 41–63. Minneapolis: University of Minnesota.

———. 1996. *Challenging Codes: Collective Action in the Information Age.* Cambridge University Press.

Mische, Ann. 2008. *Partisan Publics: Communication and Contention Across Brazilian Youth Activist Networks.* Princeton: Princeton University Press.

———. 2009. "Projects and Possibilities: Researching Futures in Action." *Sociological Forum* 24 (3): 694–704.

Muller, James, and Charles Kenney. 2004. *Keep the Faith, Change the Church: The Battle by Catholics for the Soul of Their Church.* Emmaus, PA: Rodale.

Munson, Ziad. 2009. *The Making of Pro-life Activists: How Social Movement Mobilization Works.* Chicago: University of Chicago Press.

Nepstad, Sharon Erickson. 2001. "Creating Transnational Solidarity: The Use of Narrative in the US-Central American Peace Movement." *Mobilization* 6 (1): 21–36.

———. 2004. *Convictions of the Soul: Religion, Culture, and Agency in the Central American Solidarity Movement.* New York: Oxford University Press.

———. 2008. *Religion and War Resistance in the Plowshares Peace Movement.* New York: Oxford University Press.

O'Connor, Thomas H. 1998. *Boston Catholics: A History of the Church and Its People.* Boston: Northeastern University Press, 1998.

Olick, Jeffrey K. 2007. *The Politics of Regret: On Collective Memory and Historical Responsibility.* New York: Routledge.

Orsi, Robert. 1985. *The Madonna of 115th Street: Faith and Community in Italian Harlem, 1880–1950.* New Haven, CT: Yale University Press.

O'Toole, James. 2008. *The Faithful: A History of Catholics in American.* Cambridge, MA: Belknap Press.

Owens, Lynn. 2008. *Cracking Under Pressure: Narrating the Decline of the Amsterdam Squatters' Movement.* University Park: Pennsylvania State University Press.

Pace, Enzo. 2007. "Religion as Communication: The Changing Shape of Catholicism in Europe." In *Everyday Religion: Observing Modern Religious Lives*, edited by Nancy T. Ammerman, 37–50. New York: Oxford University Press.

Palacios, Joseph M. 2007. *The Catholic Social Imagination: Activism and the Just Society in Mexico and the United States*. Chicago: University of Chicago Press.

Passy, Florence, and Marco Guigni. 2000. "Life-Spheres, Networks, and Sustained Participation in Social Movements: A Phenomenological Approach to Political Commitment." *Sociological Forum* 15 (1): 117–44.

Pennebaker, James W., and Becky L. Banasik. 1997. "On the Creation and Maintenance of Collective Memory: History as Social Psychology." In *Collective Memory of Political Events: Social Psychological Perspectives*, edited by James W. Pennebacker, Dario Paez, and Bernard Rimé, 3–19. Mahwah: Lawrence Erlbaum.

Pettinicchio, David. 2012. "Institutional Activism: Reconsidering the Insider/Outsider Dichotomy." *Sociology Compass* 6, no. 6 (June 2012): 499–510.

Polletta, Francesca. 1998. "Contending Stories: Narrative in Social Movements." *Qualitative Sociology* 21 (4): 419–46.

———. 2002. *Freedom is an Endless Meeting: Democracy in American Social Movements*. Chicago: University of Chicago Press.

———. 2006. *It Was Like a Fever: Storytelling in Protest and Politics*. Chicago: University of Chicago Press.

Polletta, Francesca, and James Jasper. 2001. "Collective Identity and Social Movements." *Annual Review of Sociology* 27:283–305.

Pope, Stephen J. 2004. "Catholic Social Thought and the American Experience." In *American Catholics and Civic Engagement: A Distinctive Voice*, vol. 1, *American Catholics in the Public Square*, edited by Margaret O'Brien Steinfels, 26–41. Lanham: Rowman & Littlefield.

Raeburn, Nicole A. 2004. *Changing Corporate America from Inside Out: Lesbian and Gay Workplace Rights*. Minneapolis: University of Minnesota Press.

Reger, Jo. 2012. *Everywhere and Nowhere: Contemporary Feminism in the United States*. New York: Oxford University Press.

Robnett, Belinda. 1996. *How Long? How Long? African-American Women in the Struggle for Civil Rights*. New York: Oxford University Press.

Roth, Benita. 2004. *Separate Roads to Feminism: Black, Chicana, and White Feminist Movements in America's Second Wave*. New York: Cambridge University Press.

Sampson, Edward E. 1993. *Celebrating the Other: A Dialogic Account of Human Nature*. Boulder: Westview.

Santoro, Wayne, and Gail M. McGuire. 1997. "Social Movement Insiders: The Impact of Institutional Activists on Affirmative Action and Comparable Worth Policies." *Social Problems* 44 (4):503–19.

Schuck, Michael J. 2013. "The Catholic Church and the Movements: Revisiting the History of Catholic Social Thought." *Journal of Catholic Social Thought* 10 (2): 241–57.

Schutz, Alfred. 1973. "Choosing Among Projects of Actions." In *Collected Papers*, vol. 1, edited and introduced by Maurice Natanson, 67–96. The Hague: Marintus Nijhoff.

———. 1970. *Alfred Schutz on Phenomenology and Social Relationships*. Edited by Helmut R. Wagner. Chicago: University of Chicago Press.

Scott, David. 2009. "Preface: The Paradox of Beginnings." *Small Axe* 26 (13): vii–xiv.

Seidman, Steve. 1997. *Difference Troubles*. Oxford: Blackwell.

Seitz, John. 2011. *No Closure: Catholic Practice and Boston's Parish Shutdowns*. Cambridge, MA: Harvard University Press.

Sewell, William H., Jr. 2005. *Logics of History: Social Theory and Social Transformation*. Chicago: University of Chicago Press.

Silbey, Jessica. 2010. "Comparative Tales of Origins and Access: Intellectual Property and the Rhetoric of Social Change." *Case Western Reserve Law Review* 61 (1): 195–267.

Simmel, Georg. 1955. *Conflict and The Web of Group Affiliations*. Translated by Kurt Wolff and Reinhard Bendix. New York: The Free Press.

Smith, Dorothy E. 2005. *Institutional Ethnography: A Sociology for People*. Walnut Creek: AltaMira Press.

Smith, Jonathan, Paul Flowers, and Michael Larkin. 2009. *Interpretative Phenomenological Analysis: Theory, Method and Research*. London: Sage.

Smithey, Lee A. 2009. "Social Movement Strategy, Tactics, and Collective Identity." *Sociology Compass* 3 (4): 658–71.

Snow, David A. 2001. "Collective Identity and Expressive Forms." In *International Encyclopedia of the Social & Behavioral Sciences*, vol. 4, edited by Neil J. Smelser and Paul B. Baltes, 2212–19. Amsterdam: Elsevier.

———. 2004. "Framing Processes, Ideology and Discursive Fields." In *The Blackwell Companion to Social Movements*, edited by David A. Snow, Sarah A. Soule, and Hanspeter Kriesi, 380–413. Oxford: Blackwell.

———. 2013. "Identity Dilemmas, Discursive Fields, Identity Work and Mobilization: Clarifying the Identity/Movement Nexus." In *The Future of Social Movement Research*, edited by Bert Klandermans, Jacquelien van Stekelenburg, and C. M. Roggeband, 263–80. Minneapolis: University of Minnesota Press.

Snow, David A., and Robert D. Benford. 2000. "Framing Processes and Social Movements: An Overview and Assessment." *Annual Review of Sociology* 26: 611–39.

Snow, David A., and Doug McAdam. 2000. "Identity Work Processes in the Context of Social Movements: Clarifying the Identity/Movement Nexus." In *Self, Identity, and Social Movements*, edited by Sheldon Stryker, Timothy J. Owens, and Robert W. White, 41–67. Minneapolis: University of Minnesota Press.

Snow, David A., and Michael Mulcahy. 2001. "Space, Politics, and the Survival Strategies of the Homeless." *American Behavioral Scientist* 45 (1): 149–69.

Somers, Margaret R. 1992. "Narrativity, Narrative Identity, and Social Action: Rethinking English Working-Class Formation." *Social Science History* 16 (4): 591–630.

———. 1994. "The Narrative Constitution of Identity: A Relational and Network Approach." *Theory and Society* 23 (5): 605–49.

Spickard, James V. 2005. "Ritual, Symbol, and Experience: Understanding Catholic Worker House Masses." *Sociology of Religion* 66 (4): 337–57.

Summers Effler, Erika. 2010. *Laughing Saints and Righteous Heroes: Emotional Rhythms in Social Movement Groups*. Chicago: University of Chicago Press.

Tilly, Charles. 1998. *Durable Inequality*. Berkeley: University of California Press.

———. 2008. *Contentious Performances*. Cambridge: Cambridge University Press.

Tsing, Anna. 2005. *Friction: An Ethnography of Global Connections*. Princeton: Princeton University Press.

Valocchi, Stephen. 2008. "The Importance of Being 'We': Collective Identity and the Mobilizing Work of Progressive Activists in Hartford, Connecticut." *Mobilization* 14 (1): 65–84.

van Stekelenburg, Jacquelien, and Bert Klandermans. 2007. "Individuals in Movements: A Social Psychology of Contention." In *Handbook of Social Movements Across Disciplines*, edited by Bert Klandermans and Conny Roggeband, 157–204. New York: Springer.

van Zomeren, Martijn, Russell Spears, Agneta Fisher, and Colin W. Leach. 2004. "Put Your Money Where Your Mouth Is! Explaining Collective Action Tendencies Through Group-Based Anger and Group Efficacy." *Journal of Personality and Social Psychology* 87 (5): 649–64.

———. 2008. "Toward an Integrative Social Identity Model of Collective Action: A Quantitative Research Synthesis of Three Socio-psychological Perspectives." *Psychological Bulletin* 134 (4): 504–35.

Weick, Karl. 1993. "The Collapse of Sensemaking in Organizations: The Mann Gulch Disaster." *Administrative Science Quarterly* 38 (4): 628–52.

Weick, Karl, Kathleen M. Sutcliffe, and David Obstfeld. 2005. "Organization and the Problem of Sensemaking." *Organizational Science* 16 (4): 409–21.

Welch, Michael. 2010. "Pastoral Power as Penal Resistance: Foucault and the Groupe d'Information sur les Prisons." *Punishment and Society* 12 (1): 47–63.

Wertsch, James V. 2002. *Voices of Collective Remembering*. Cambridge: Cambridge University Press.

White, James B. 1990. *Justice as Translation: An Essay in Cultural and Legal Criticism*. Chicago: University of Chicago Press.

Whittier, Nancy. 1995. *Feminist Generations: The Persistence of the Radical Women's Movement*. Philadelphia: Temple University Press.

———. 1996. "Political Generations, Micro-Cohorts, and the Transformation of Social Movements." *American Sociological Review* 62 (5): 760–78.

———. 2002. "Meaning and Structure in Social Movements." In *Social Movements: Identity, Culture and the State*, edited by David S. Meyer, Nancy Whittier, and Belinda Robnett, 289–307. Oxford: Oxford University Press.

Wilde, Melissa J. 2007. *Vatican II: A Sociological Analysis of Religious Change*. Princeton: Princeton University Press.

Wood, Lesley. 2012. *Direct Action, Deliberation and Diffusion: Collective Action After the WTO Protests in Seattle*. Cambridge: Cambridge University Press.

Wood, Richard L. 2002. *Faith in Action: Religion, Race, and Democratic Organizing in America*. Chicago: University of Chicago Press.

Yukich, Grace. 2010. "Boundary Work in Inclusive Religious Groups: Constructing Identity at the New York Catholic Worker." *Sociology of Religion* 71 (2): 172–96.

Zald, Mayer N., and John D. McCarthy. 1987. *Social Movements in an Organizational Society*. New Brunswick: Transaction Books.

Zerubavel, Evitar. 2005. *Time Maps: Collective Memory and the Shape of the Past*. Chicago: University of Chicago Press.

Index